TOPICS

- Stores and Transfers
- Energy Conservation and Efficiency
- Kinetic Energy
- Gravitational Potential Energy
- Elastic Potential Energy
- Power
- Heat Transfer
- Energy Resources

- Drawing Circuits
- Current and Charge
- Potential Difference, Current and Resistance
- I-V Characteristics
- LDRs and Thermistors
- Series Circuits
- Parallel Circuits
- Series and Parallel Circuits
- Electrical Power
- Energy Transfer in Circuits
- Static Electricity

- Density
- Specific Heat Capacity 1
- Specific Heat Capacity 2
- Specific Latent Heat

- Atoms and Isotopes
- Radioactive Decay
- Half-life
- Fission and Fusion

- Identifying Forces
- Free Body Diagrams
- Resolving Forces
- Work Done
- Springs
- Moments
- Pressure at a Surface
- Pressure at a Depth in Fluids
- Speed
- Velocity
- Acceleration
- Distance-time Graphs
- Velocity-time Graphs
- Equations of Motion
- Newton's Second Law
- Stopping Distances
- Momentum
- Conservation of Momentum

- Wave Calculations
- Reflection
- Ultrasound Scanning
- Electromagnetic Waves
- Refraction
- Convex (Converging) Lenses
- Concave (Diverging) Lenses
- Colour

- Magnetic Fields
- The Motor Effect
- Generator Effect
- Transformers 1
- Transformers 2

- Lifecycle of Stars
- The Big Bang

HOW TO USE THIS BOOK

The idea is pretty simple – answer the questions in this workbook.

1. Have a go at the questions:
   - A quick **diagram** can often be useful
   - Identify the **quantities** in the question
   - Write down the correct **equation**
   - Show your **working** out
   - Round your answer to an appropriate number of **significant figures**
   - Don't forget the **units**

2. Mark your work:
   - Use the **answers** in the **back of this book**.

   - If you need any extra guidance, scan the QR code or visit **GCSEPhysicsOnline**.com to view videos that explain how to answer all the questions.

The content in this workbook is not exam board specific, meaning it can be used by students studying AQA, Edexcel, OCR, WJEC, CCEA, CIE IGCSE, Edexcel IGCSE and many more.

Furthermore, this book is suitable for both Foundation and Higher tier students taking Combined / Double / Trilogy Science or the Triple/ Separate Physics course. Make sure you are familiar with your course specification, focusing on questions that are only relevant to your exams.

PREMIUM PLAN

Find the support you require whenever you need it. To access all the videos that explain the answers in this workbook you can sign up for an individual **Premium Plan**. This allows you to see hundreds of exclusive additional videos and resources covering the entire GCSE, all organised by exam board and topic.

It's a simple, affordable, one-off payment that lasts for your entire GCSE course.

School Subscriptions are also available for your whole class – just ask your teacher to sign up for this.

GCSEPhysicsOnline.com/**premium**

On the website you'll find a section like this for every set of questions.

Download an extra printable sheet if needed

Need more support? Watch the video to see a full explanation of the answers.

Energy

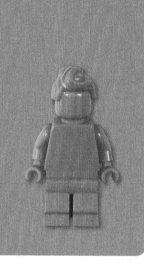

GCSE
ENERGY STORES AND TRANSFERS

Energy can be stored and transferred in different ways.

1. Write down the unit for measuring energy.

2. Write down eight different energy stores.

    -
    -
    -
    -
    -
    -
    -
    -

3. Write down the four main types of energy transfer between stores. (Hint: HERM)

    -
    -
    -
    -

4. A teddy bear is thrown vertically upwards from the ground. It has an initial kinetic energy of 68 J.

    a. As the bear travels upwards, describe what happens to the value of energy in the kinetic store

    b. The kinetic energy is transferred to a different store of energy, write down the name of this store

    c. Write down the name of the type of energy transfer responsible for transferring the kinetic energy to this new energy store

    d. Write down the value of energy in this new store when the bear is at the top of its flight path (at the highest point)

5. For the following examples, name the store(s) that the energy is stored in:

   a. A bow that has been pulled back

   b. The nucleus of an oxygen atom

   c. The south poles of two bar magnets being held close together

   d. A hot hotdog

6. For the following examples, name the initial and final energy stores as well as the method responsible for transferring energy from the initial to the final store:

   a. The Sun heating up the Earth

   b. A travelling bullet hitting a target

   c. A burger being cooked on a charcoal barbeque

7. Describe the changes in the way energy is stored for a petrol car accelerating from rest to a velocity of 60 mph on a level road. Assume no energy is lost to the surroundings.

8. Describe the changes in the way energy is stored for an elastic band that is stretched and fired vertically upwards. Assume no energy is lost to the surroundings.

9. Describe the changes in the way energy is stored for a pole vaulter, starting at rest, accelerating, then using a bendy pole to get over a high bar.

GCSE
ENERGY CONSERVATION AND EFFICIENCY

Energy cannot be created or destroyed.

efficiency = useful output energy transfer / total input energy transfer

1. Write down the name given to energy that is not usefully transferred.

2. Write down two different ways efficiency can be displayed in.

3. Describe what happens to energy that is not usefully transferred, including the store it is most commonly transferred to.

4. Write down another version of the equation for efficiency concerning power.

   efficiency =

5. Calculate the percentage efficiency of a machine that has:

   a. A total energy input of 40 J and a useful energy output of 22 J

   b. A total energy input of 124 J and a useful energy output of 43.4 J

   c. A total power input of 2.4 W and a useful power output of 0.96 W

6. Explain why electric heaters can have very high efficiencies.

7. Explain what is meant by thermal conductivity, giving examples of good and bad thermal conductors.

8. An ultra-ultra-bouncy ball is dropped from a height of 12.0 m. After it bounces once, the ball reaches a height of 10.8 m.

   a. Calculate the efficiency of the ball as a percentage

   b. Calculate the height reached after the ball bounces i) twice, ii) three times and iii) six times

      i.

      ii.

      iii.

9. A rocket's engine uses 170 kJ worth of fuel in the first stage of taking off. The rocket itself gains 36.0 kJ of kinetic energy as well as 32.0 kJ of gravitational potential energy.

   a. Calculate the efficiency of the rocket's engine

   Before the next take-off, the rocket's engine has its efficiency increased by 10%.

   b. Calculate the new useful output energy transfer

10. An electric car is used to deliver pizzas. The car's efficiency is 0.73 and its useful power output is 8.7 kW.

    a. Calculate the power input

    The power input is increased by 25% but this decreases the efficiency to 0.63.

    b. Calculate the new useful power output. Comment if the useful power output is now greater than it was before

GCSE
KINETIC ENERGY

The energy stored by moving objects.

kinetic energy = ½ x mass x velocity²

1. Write the equation in symbols and name the units that each of the three variables in the equation are measured in.

2. Calculate the kinetic energy of:

   a. A 3.0 kg mass moving at 4.0 m/s

   b. A 6.0 kg mass moving at 4.0 m/s

   c. A 3.0 kg mass moving at 8.0 m/s

   d. Compare what happens to the kinetic energy of an object when its mass is doubled versus what happens when its velocity is doubled

3. Rearrange the equation to i) make **m** the subject, then ii) rearrange to make **v** the subject.

   i)   ii)

4. Fill in the table with the missing values (to 3 sf).

Kinetic Energy (J)	Mass (kg)	Velocity (m/s)	Calculations
	5.00	5.00	
	5.00	10.0	
243	6.00		
243		11.0	
243	0.600		
42.0		4.63	

gcsephysicsonline.com/**kinetic**

5. A tennis ball has a mass of 58 g and is served at 42 m/s.

   a. Calculate the kinetic energy stored by the ball as it leaves the tennis racket

The ball is hit harder such that it stores twice as much kinetic energy.

   b. Calculate how fast the ball would need to be travelling

A baseball has a mass of 160 g and stores the same kinetic energy as a tennis ball that is travelling at 50 m/s.

   c. Calculate how fast the baseball would need to be travelling

6. The International Space Station (ISS) orbits at 7.66 km/s and has a mass of 420 tonnes.

   a. Calculate the ISS's kinetic energy   (1 tonne = 1000 kg)

A 4.30 tonne geostationary communications satellite orbits at 3.07 km/s.

   b. Calculate the satellite's kinetic energy

   c. Compare how much energy is stored by the ISS to the communication satellite, give your answer as a ratio

An asteroid travels at the same speed as the ISS in part a. (7.66 km/s), but possesses the same kinetic energy as the satellite in part b.

   d. Calculate the asteroid's mass

GCSE
GRAVITATIONAL POTENTIAL ENERGY

The energy stored by objects in a gravitational field.

gravitational potential energy = mass x gravitational field strength x height

1. Name the units that each of the four variables in the equation are measured in.

2. Write down the value of Earth's gravitational field strength (to one decimal place).

3. Calculate, using your answer to question 2, the gravitational potential energy of:

    a. A 4.0 kg mass, 7.9 m above the Earth's surface

    b. A 3.0 kg mass, 16 m above the Earth's surface

4. i) Rearrange the equation to make **m** the subject, ii) rearrange to make **h** the subject and iii) rearrange to make **g** the subject.

    i)   ii)   iii)

5. Fill in the table with the missing values (to 2 sf).

E_p (J)	m (kg)	g (N/Kg)	h (m)	Calculations
	5.0	9.8	3.0	
	7.5	9.8	28	
350	10	1.6		
200	6.0	9.8		
810		9.8	19	
240		1.6	0.6	
34	0.2		6.3	
89	18		1.5	

physics online

6. A cannonball has a mass of 13 kg and is fired vertically upwards from the surface of the Earth to a height of 27 m. (use g = 9.8 N/kg at the surface of Earth.)

   a. Calculate the cannonball's maximum gravitational potential energy

The cannonball is fired upwards such that it stores double the maximum gravitational potential energy.

   b. Calculate how high the ball is fired

7. An alien flies at a height of 123 m above its home planet's surface. The alien has a mass of 12 kg and stores 790 J of gravitational potential energy. Calculate the value of 'g' for this planet.

8. An astronaut on the surface of the Moon has a mass of 75 kg. They pick up a rock which has a mass of 1.5 kg. (The value of g on the Moon = 1.6 N/kg.)

   a. Calculate the increase in gravitational potential energy of the astronaut holding the rock if they jump a height of 1.2 m

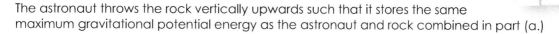

The astronaut throws the rock vertically upwards such that it stores the same maximum gravitational potential energy as the astronaut and rock combined in part (a.)

   b. Calculate the rock's increase in height

The astronaut picks up another rock and throws it vertically upwards. This rock reaches the same height as in (b.) but stores 35 J more gravitational potential energy than in (a.)

   c. Calculate this rock's mass

GCSE
ELASTIC POTENTIAL ENERGY

The energy stored by objects which have been elastically deformed (stretched or compressed within the limit of proportionality).

$$E_e = \tfrac{1}{2} k e^2$$

1. Write down the equation using words rather than symbols and name the units.

2. Calculate the elastic potential energy stored by:

   a. A spring with a spring constant of 72.0 N/m that is extended by 0.300 m

   b. A spring with a spring constant of 72.0 N/m that is extended by 0.150 m

   c. A spring with a spring constant of 36.0 N/m that is extended by 0.300 m

   d. Compare what happens to the elastic potential energy of a spring when its extension is doubled versus when its spring constant is doubled

3. i) Rearrange the equation to make **k** the subject, then ii) rearrange to make **e** the subject.

   i)   ii)

4. Fill in the table with the missing values (to 2 sf).

E_e (J)	k (N/m)	Extension (m)	Calculations
	5.0	1.2	
	17	0.90	
110		0.40	
280		0.60	
240	78		

physics online

5. A bird feeder is suspended on the end of a spring. The spring has a spring constant of 129 N/m and has an original length of 12.0 cm. When the bird feeder, which is full of bird food, is hung from the spring, the spring extends to 17.0 cm.

   a. Calculate the extension of the spring

   b. Calculate the elastic potential energy stored in the spring

   Over the course of a few days, all the bird food is eaten. The elastic potential energy of the spring is now a quarter of what it was in part (b.)

   c. Calculate the new extension of the spring, and hence its final length

6. A 10 cm long spring, with a spring constant of 27 N/m, is used to reload the ball in a pinball machine. The spring is compressed by 4.0 cm by a mechanism in the machine and then let go.

   a. Calculate the elastic potential energy stored in the spring

   A new spring is fitted into the machine. It only needs to be compressed by 3.0 cm to store the same amount of elastic potential energy as the previous spring.

   b. Calculate the spring constant of this new spring

   The owner of the game wants to double the potential energy stored in this new spring.

   c. Calculate the compression of the spring needed in order to achieve this

   A child, eating a 30 cm long gummy snake which has a spring constant of 15 N/m, comes to play on the machine. The child pulls the gummy snake until its length has doubled.

      d. Calculate the elastic potential energy stored in the gummy snake assuming the gummy snake has been stretched within the limit of proportionality

GCSE
POWER

Power is the rate of transfer of energy.

power = energy transferred / time

1. Write down the equation using symbols rather than words.

2. Name the units that each of the three variables in the equation are measured in.

3. Calculate the power for:

    a. 780 J transferred over 12 s

    b. 0.30 J transferred over 0.050 s

    c. 12 kJ transferred over one minute

    d. 5.4 MJ transferred over one hour

4. Rearrange the original equation to make **E** the subject, then ii) rearrange to make **t** the subject.

    i)   ii)

5. Fill in the table with the missing values (to an appropriate number of sf).

Power (W)	Energy Transferred (J)	Time (s)	Calculations
	78.9	12.0	
760	380		
8.8	2200		
1800		0.50	
89		66	

6. A battery transfers 1.5 J of energy over 28s.

    a. Calculate the power of the battery at this time

A different batter transfers 2.3 J of energy over 34s.

    b. Calculate if this battery has a greater power than the first battery

7. An office photocopier requires a power input of 0.80 W when it is left on standby. The photocopier is left on standby overnight for 9.0 hours.

    a. Calculate how much energy is transferred by the photocopier

No one uses the office over the weekend and sometimes the lights get left on. There are four 60 W bulbs in the office that are left on from 6.00 pm on Friday to 9.00 am on Monday.

    b. Calculate the total energy transferred in this time by the four bulbs

8. An oven has a power rating of 2.4 kW. It takes half an hour to cook a fillet of fish.

    a. Assuming all the energy is transferred to the fish, calculate its increase in thermal energy

    b. Calculate the power of a different oven, one that transfers the same amount of energy but in 4 minutes less

9. A crane uses a motor to lift heavy objects. The crane takes exactly 20 seconds to lift an object with a mass of 520 kg a height of 18 m.

    Calculate the power of the crane's motor, assuming that all the energy is transferred usefully into lifting the object

GCSE
HEAT TRANSFER

A common process for heat transfer is conduction.

1. Write down how closely-packed particles are in a) a solid, b) a liquid and c) a gas.

    a.

    b.

    c.

2. Describe what happens to the motion of the particles in; a) a solid, b) a liquid and c) a gas as the particles' temperature is increased.

    a.

    b.

    c.

3. Describe how heat is transferred via conduction.

4. Using your answer to question 1, explain why solids are generally better thermal conductors than gases.

5. Most solids are made of neatly packed neutral atoms. Describe why metals are different.

6. Explain why your answer to question 5 means that metals are generally better thermal conductors than most solids.

7. Explain why copper is such a good thermal conductor.

8. A student measures the temperature of a block of plastic and a block of metal. They both have a temperature of 20 °C but the student claims the metal block feels colder. Explain why.

9. Write down the type of material that is a poor thermal conductor.

10. Write down the name given to a material's ability to thermally conduct heat.

11. Thermal conduction transfers thermal energy (heat). Explain why insulators can improve efficiency.

12. Double glazed windows have two panes of glass separated by a sealed layer of gas. Explain why double glazed windows are better insulators than single glazed windows.

13. Explain why the roof of a house has fibreglass insulation in it and why the ground floor does not have the same type of insulation underneath it.

GCSE
ENERGY RESOURCES

Energy can be stored in different ways and in different objects and materials. Energy can be transferred from these stores for use in transport, heating and our homes.

1. Name as many non-renewable energy sources as you can.

2. Name as many renewable energy sources as you can.

3. Describe the main difference between non-renewable and renewable energy sources and how this makes renewable energy sources better for the planet.

4. Briefly explain how a conventional power station converts the chemical energy in the fuels it burns until it is transferred electrically.

5. The National Grid has to cope with balancing supply with a rapidly changing demand. Describe why traditional power stations are useful for keeping up with demand.

6. Write down the main drawbacks with traditional fossil fuel power stations.

7. Explain why some people think nuclear power stations are better for the environment than traditional power stations and why some think they are worse.

8. Wind turbines also use a turbine to produce electricity. Explain how the design of a wind turbine means that no fuel is needed.

9. Write down the problem with solar panels that wind turbines also share.

10. Explain the benefit of hydroelectric power stations in terms of storing surplus energy.

11. Write down the problem with hydroelectric power stations that geothermal power stations also share.

12. Wave power and tidal power are both renewable energy sources that also harness the power of water. Describe how i) waves and ii) tides can be harnessed.

13. Describe the problem harnessing tidal power poses to local wildlife.

Electricity

GCSE
DRAWING CIRCUITS

Circuit drawings are a simple way of displaying the workings of an electrical circuit, with each electrical component corresponding to its own symbol.

1. Sketch the circuit symbol for the following electrical components:

    a. A cell

    b. A wire

    c. A voltmeter

    d. An ammeter

    e. An open switch

    f. A filament lightbulb

    g. A resistor

    h. An LED

    i. A battery

2. Write down any pieces of equipment that would be useful in drawing circuit diagrams.

3. Define the difference between a series circuit and a parallel circuit.

4. Name a component that must be connected in series and another that must be connected in parallel.

5. Draw two different circuits that could both connect a bulb, a resistor and a switch to a battery.

6. Draw a parallel circuit with three loops, one loop with a switch and a bulb, another loop with an LED and a resistor and another with an ammeter and a variable resistor.

7. The circuit diagram below is both incorrect and badly drawn. Identify all the things that are wrong with it (there are five).

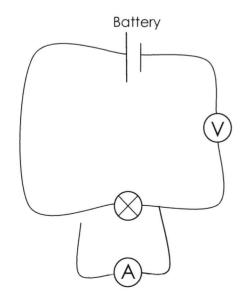

Battery

gcsephysicsonline.com/**circuits-symbols**

GCSE
CURRENT AND CHARGE

Current is the rate of flow of electric charge.

$$I = Q/t$$

1. Write down the equation using words rather than symbols and name the units that each of the three variables in the equation are measured in.

2. i) Rearrange the equation to make **Q** the subject, then ii) rearrange to make **t** the subject.

   i)   ii)

3. In a circuit, charged particles flow through wires when a potential difference (voltage) is applied. Write down the name of these particles.

4. Conventional current flows in the opposite direction to these charged particles. Explain why.

5. Calculate the current when there is:

   a. 6.0 C of charge flowing past a point in a circuit over a period of 30 s

   b. 0.40 C of charge flowing past a point in a circuit over a period of 50 s

   c. 36 C of charge flowing past a point in a circuit over a period of 3 minutes

6. Fill in the table with the missing values.

Current (A)	Charge (C)	Time (s)	Calculations
7.9		56	
0.12		3600	
0.40	0.020		
0.0030	6.3		

7. A student builds a simple electrical circuit. However, the reading on their ammeter is 0.0 A.

   a. Provided the ammeter isn't broken, write down a possible reason why the current might be zero

The issue is fixed. However, this time the reading on the ammeter is negative.

   b. Explain why this might be the case

The student rewires the circuit so that the ammeter reads a positive value of 1.4 A. The student disconnects the circuit after 25 s.

   c. Calculate the charge that has flowed through the ammeter

The student adds another power source such that the time it takes for the same amount of charge to flow through the circuit is 18 s.

   d. Calculate the reading that would display on the ammeter when the circuit was connected

8. A conventional oven requires a current of approximately 18 A. While cooking a meal, 32 400 C of charge is transferred through the oven.

   a. Calculate the time the oven takes to cook the meal

For a different meal, the oven cooks it in 10 minutes less.

   b. Calculate the total charge that has flowed through the oven for this meal

9. In a small laptop, 450 mC is transferred through its circuit every minute.

   a. Calculate the current in the computer

The battery in the laptop stores 135 C of charge.

   b. Calculate how long the battery would last

GCSE
POTENTIAL DIFFERENCE, RESISTANCE AND CURRENT

The potential difference (or voltage) is a measure of how much energy the charged particles in a circuit have per unit charge. It is also related to current and resistance.

$$V = IR$$

1. Write down the equation using words rather than symbols and name the units that each of the three variables in the equation are measured in.

2. Ammeters are connected in series because they measure the current flowing through the circuit. Explain why voltmeters are connected in parallel.

3. i) Rearrange the equation to make **I** the subject, then ii) rearrange to make **R** the subject.

   i)   ii)

4. Calculate the potential difference across:

   a. A 4.0 Ω resistor with 2.5 A through it

   b. A 7.5 Ω bulb with 0.20 A through it

   c. A 1.4 kΩ resistor with 2.9 mA through it

5. Fill in the table with the missing values.

Voltage (V)	Current (A)	Resistance (Ω)	Calculations
12		0.40	
230		4600	
9.0	0.30		
1.5	0.30		

physics online

6. Mains electricity in your house has a potential difference of 230 V. A hairdryer, with a resistance of 46 Ω, is plugged in.

   a. Calculate the current flowing through the hairdryer

A hair straightener is plugged into the same mains supply which causes a current of 2.3 A to flow.

   b. Calculate the electrical resistance of the hair straighteners

7. A scientist builds a simple series circuit made of a 9.0 V battery and two resistors, R_1 and R_2. R_1 has a resistance equal to the hairdryer and R_2 has a resistance equal to the hair straighteners from the previous question.

   a. Draw the circuit and add one ammeter and two voltmeters in appropriate places

   b. Calculate the current flowing through both R_1 and R_2

   c. Calculate the potential difference across R_1 and potential difference across R_2

8. A large lithium-ion battery holds 2.1 kC of charge. When connected in series to a 300 Ω resistor, the battery transfers all of its charge in exactly one day.

   Calculate the potential difference across the battery

The I-V characteristics of an electrical component refer to the relationship between the current flowing through and the potential difference across the component.

1. Write down the equation for resistance in terms of current and potential difference (voltage).

2. Define what an ohmic conductor is.

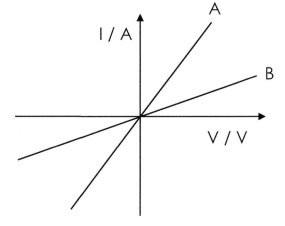

3. The graph on the right shows the I-V characteristics of two fixed resistors, A and B.

   a. Write down if A is an ohmic conductor

   b. Explain which of the two resistors has a greater resistance and why

4. A filament bulb is not an ohmic conductor. This means its resistance is not constant and hence its I-V graph is not a straight line.

   a. Sketch the I-V graph for a filament bulb on the axes on the right

   b. Describe in detail how a filament bulb produces light

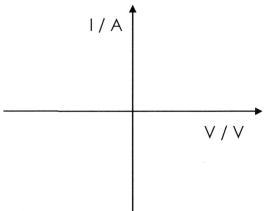

   c. Explain in detail why a filament bulb is not an ohmic conductor

5. A diode is unlike other electrical components for one main reason.

   a. Write down what property makes a diode special

   b. Sketch the I-V characteristic graph for a diode on the axes on the right

   c. Write down what LED stands for

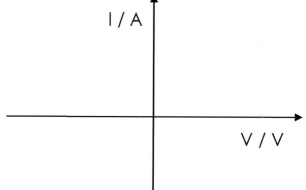

6. Below is a graph showing the relationship between the current through a resistor and the potential resistance across it. Calculate the resistance of the resistor.

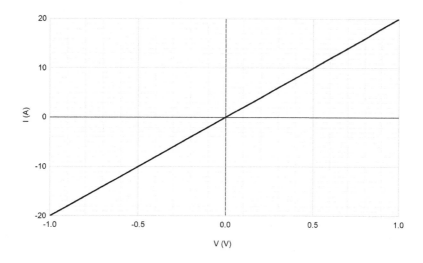

7. Below is a graph showing the relationship between the current through a different component and the potential resistance across it. Calculate the resistance of the bulb when the potential difference across it is -4.0 V.

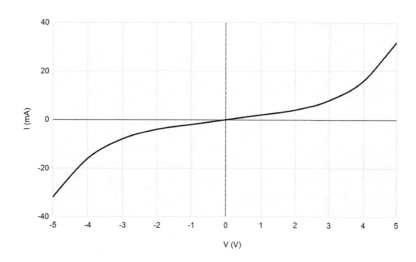

GCSE
LDRS AND THERMISTORS

LDRs and thermistors are both types of variable resistors. LDR is short for light dependent resistor - their resistance is dependent on light intensity whereas a thermistor's resistance is dependent on temperature.

1. Draw the symbols for i) an LDR and ii) a thermistor.

    i.   ii.

2. Describe the relationship between the resistance of an LDR and the light intensity.

3. Sketch and label a graph showing the relationship between the resistance of an LDR and light intensity on the axes below. Remember to label the axes.

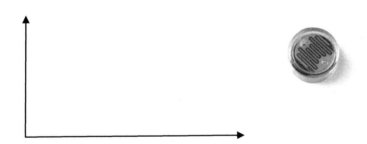

4. Describe the relationship between the resistance of a thermistor and temperature.

5. Sketch a graph showing the relationship between the resistance of a thermistor and temperature on the axes below. Remember to label the axes.

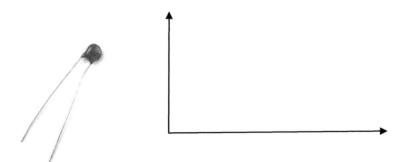

6. LDRs can be used in street lights as a sensor to turn the lights on and off. The diagram below shows a possible circuit set-up for a street light.

a. Describe how the circuit on the right turns the street light on when it gets dark and turns it off when it gets light

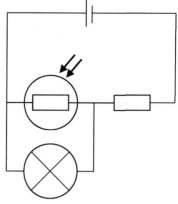

b. Below is a graph showing the relationship between resistance and light intensity for the LDR used in the circuit above. The circuit is designed to turn on the light when the light intensity falls beneath 1000 lux.

Determine the resistance of the LDR when the light switches on

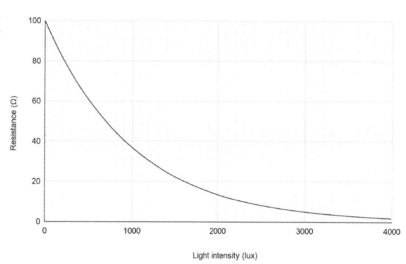

Light intensity (lux)

Thermistors can be used in a similar way but instead they can be used to sense when an object gets too hot or too cold. Below is a graph showing the relationship between resistance and temperature for a thermistor that is connected to a 9.0 V supply.

c. Calculate the change in current flowing through the thermistor as the temperature is increased from 10 °C to 50 °C

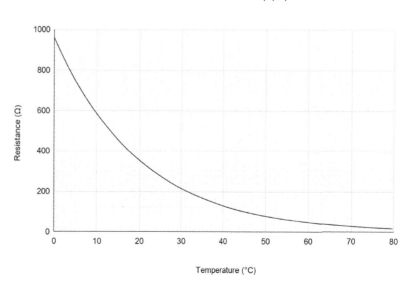

Temperature (°C)

 **GCSE**
SERIES CIRCUITS

Series circuits are when two or more electrical components are connected by wire to form a single conducting loop.

1. Identify the six circuit symbols drawn below.

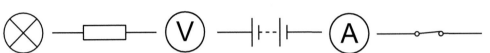

2. Identify any electrical components above that should only be connected in series.

3. Draw a circuit that has four 1.5 V cells connected to a diode, resistor and filament lamp in series. Include an ammeter that could be used to record the current through the resistor.

4. A simple series circuit is set up: a 6.0 V battery, a filament bulb and a resistor are connected in a single loop. The battery causes 72 C of charge to flow through the circuit every minute.

   a. Draw a circuit diagram

   b. Calculate the current through the circuit

The filament bulb has a resistance of 2.0 Ω and the resistor has a resistance of 3.0 Ω.

    c. Calculate the potential difference across:

        i. The filament bulb

        ii. The resistor

    d. Check the values of potential difference for the electrical components are correct by comparing them to the potential difference across the battery

    e. Calculate the total resistance of the circuit

5. An 8.0 V cell is connected in series to three identical resistors: $R_1 = R_2 = R_3 = 3.0$ Ω and an ammeter.

    a. Calculate the total resistance of the circuit

    b. Calculate the current flowing through every point in the circuit

    One of the resistors is removed and replaced by a 6.0 Ω resistor.

    c. Calculate the new current in the circuit

    d. Compare the new current and resistance to the initial values

physics
online

gcsephysicsonline.com/**series-parallel**

GCSE
PARALLEL CIRCUITS

Parallel circuits occur when two or more electrical components are connected to form two or more conducting loops in a circuit.

1. State the effect on the overall resistance of adding a resistor in parallel to any circuit.

2. The current is the same everywhere in a parallel circuit (if false, explain).

   - True   • False

3. In a parallel circuit, the potential difference across each loop is the same and equal to the potential difference across the cell or battery (if false, explain).

   - True   • False

4. Voltmeters must be connected to a circuit in parallel (if false, explain).

   - True   • False

5. A 10.0 Ω resistor and a filament bulb, with resistance 5.0 Ω, are connected in parallel to a 5.0 V cell.

   a. Draw the circuit

   b. Write down the potential difference across both the resistor and the bulb

   c. Calculate the current through i) the resistor and ii) the bulb

      i.

      ii.

   d. Hence calculate the total current flowing through the cell

   e. Calculate the total resistance, R_T, of the circuit

6. In both circuits below, the potential difference across the battery is 10.0 V and each bulb has a resistance of 5.0 Ω.

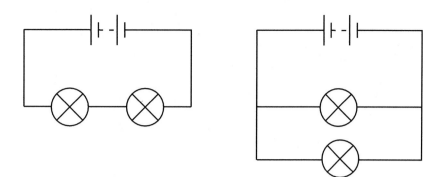

Calculate:

a. The total resistance of the bulbs in series and the combined resistance of the bulbs in parallel

b. The potential difference across each individual bulb

c. The current through each individual bulb

d. Comment on the differences in the values of resistance, potential difference and current between the parallel and series circuits.

Series and parallel circuits behave differently when we compare the current and potential difference in each part of the circuit.

1. Calculate the current at the points in the circuits below.

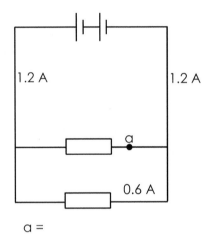

a =

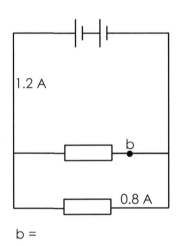

b =

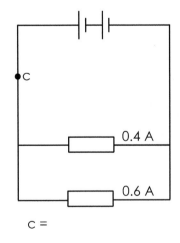

c =

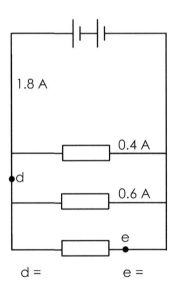

d =   e =

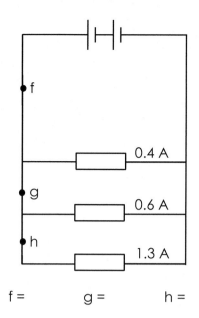

f =   g =   h =

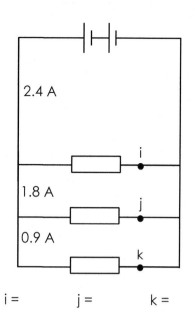

i =   j =   k =

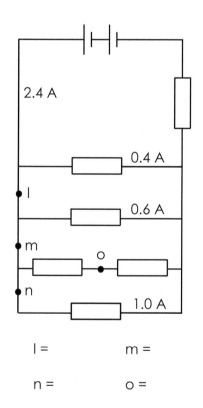

l =   m =

n =   o =

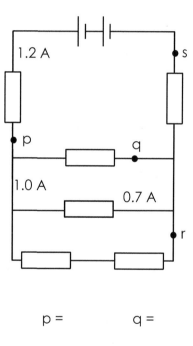

p =   q =

r =   s =

2. Calculate the potential difference (voltage) across each of these resistors in the circuits below.

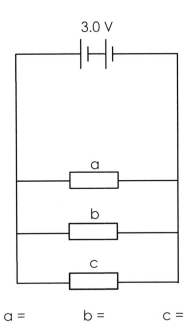

3.0 V

a

b

c

a =   b =   c =

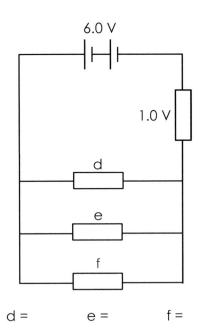

6.0 V

1.0 V

d

e

f

d =   e =   f =

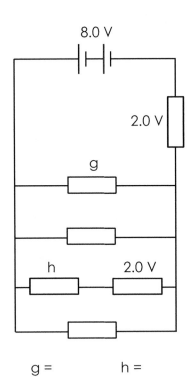

8.0 V

2.0 V

g

h   2.0 V

g =   h =

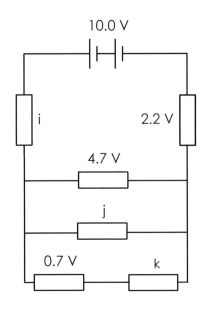

10.0 V

i   2.2 V

4.7 V

j

0.7 V   k

i =   j =   k =

3. Calculate the missing values in the circuits below.

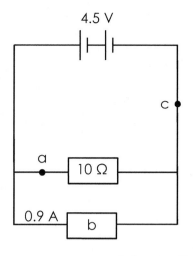

a =   A (current)

b =   Ω (resistance)

c =   A (current)

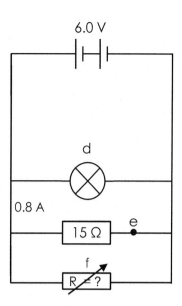

d =   V (potential difference)

e =   A (current)

f =   Ω (resistance)

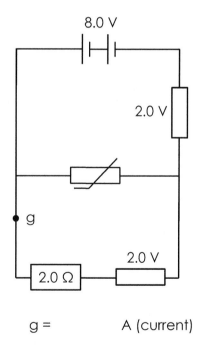

g =   A (current)

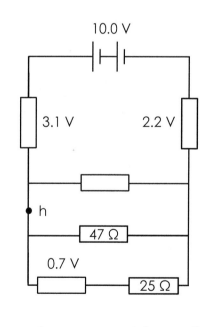

h =   A (current)

GCSE
ELECTRICAL POWER

Both an increase in the current through a circuit and the potential difference across a circuit increase the rate of energy transfer. Hence they both increase the power of the circuit – the energy transferred per second.

$$P = VI$$

1. Write down the equation using words rather than symbols and name the units that each of the three variables in the equation are measured in.

2. Calculate the power when there is:

    a. A current of 0.60 A and a potential difference of 12 V

    b. A potential difference of 0.20 V and a current of 800 mA

3. i) Rearrange the equation to make **V** the subject, then ii) rearrange to make **I** the subject.

    i.   ii.

4. Write down the equation for potential difference in terms of current and resistance.

5. Write down the equations for power in terms of i) potential difference and resistance, then ii) current and resistance.

    i.   ii.

6. Fill in the table with the missing values.

Power (W)	Voltage (V)	Current (A)	Calculations
	80	0.015	
100		2.5	
12		1.2	
45	9.0		
8.2	12		

physics online

gcsephysicsonline.com/**electrical-power**

7. A 150 W games console is plugged into a mains electricity supply at 230 V.

   a. Calculate the current in through the console

   A student plays on the console for an hour and a half.

   b. Calculate how much energy is transferred in this time

A portable console does not require mains electricity and only needs a fraction of the power. A lithium-ion battery produces a power of 12 W with a current of 1.6A.

   c. Calculate the potential difference of the portable console's battery

8. For the circuit on the right, calculate the power dissipated by the:

   a. 30 Ω resistor

   b. 120 Ω resistor

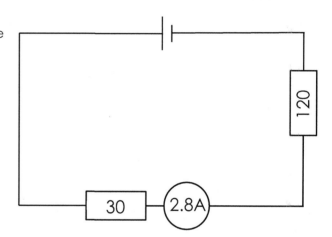

9. For the circuit on the right, calculate the power dissipated by the:

   a. 3.0 Ω resistor

   b. 10 Ω resistor

   c. 5.0 Ω resistor

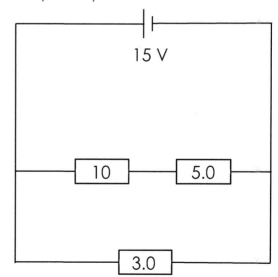

GCSE
ENERGY TRANSFER IN CIRCUITS

We know that energy transferred is equal to the power multiplied by time.
However, energy transferred is also equal to voltage multiplied by charge.

energy transferred = total charge transferred x potential difference

1. Write down the equation using symbols rather than words and name the units that each of the three variables in the equation are measured in.

2. Calculate the energy transferred when:

    a. A 12 V potential difference that transfers a charge of 50 C

    b. A 2.2 kV potential difference that transfers a charge of 0.30 C

    c. A 780 mV potential difference that transfers a charge of 3.2 kC

3. i) Rearrange the equation to make **V** the subject, then ii) rearrange to make **Q** the subject.

    i.   Ii.

4. Use your equation for **V** to provide a definition of potential difference.

5. Fill in the table with the missing values.

Energy (J)	Voltage (V)	Charge (Q)	Calculations
	90.0	2.40	
	8.20	80.0	
45 000	600		
450	60		
0.0252		0.0042	
7 200 000		9000	

6. A kettle has a power rating of 2800 W and takes 3.0 minutes to boil exactly a litre of water.

   a. Calculate how much energy is transferred to the water

The kettle is connected to mains electricity which has a potential difference of 230 V.

   b. Calculate the total amount of charge transferred

A 60W light bulb is also connected to the mains and is left on for 5 hours.

   c. Calculate if the bulb left on for 5 hours transfers more energy than the kettle does to boil **two** litres of water

7. A single 6.0 V cell powers a handheld fan. When the weather is hot, 20 office workers each have an individual fan on for the whole working day which is 8 hours. The current drawn within a single fan is 0.15 A.

   a. Calculate the energy transferred by the fans

One of the workers suggests a small air conditioning unit for the whole office would be more efficient. A small air conditioning unit requires mains electricity and draws a current of 0.30 A but only needs to be on for a total of one and a half hours throughout the day to sufficiently cool the room.

   b. Calculate if their claim is correct

GCSE
STATIC ELECTRICITY

Static electricity occurs when two objects have different charges, i.e. where one is positively charged and the other negatively charged.

1. Write down the relative charge of an electron.

2. Explain why static electricity is more common between two insulators and not two conductors.

3. When two insulators are rubbed together, one loses some of its electrons to the other. Describe the effect this has on each individual insulator.

4. Complete the following:

   Like charges _____ , opposite charges _____ .

5. If one insulator gains electrons and the other loses them, write down if the two insulators attract or repel each other.

6. Write down what surrounds every charged particle and how it might be displayed in a diagram.

7. Describe how the direction of electric field lines are determined.

8. Explain what it means when electric field lines are closer together.

9. A circular balloon is rubbed on a woolly jumper. Draw the electric field lines around the balloon below.

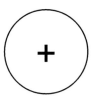

10. A teacher rubs an inflated balloon on their head. The hair on the teacher's head loses electrons and the balloon gains them.

    a. Write down which insulator is positively charged and which is negative

    b. Describe why the individual hairs on the teacher's head stand on end

11. Static electricity occurs when charged particles collect on an insulator. The insulator is very bad at conducting electricity so the charged particles have nowhere to go.

    a. Describe the dangers this may present

    b. Describe how you make an a highly charge insulator safe

Particle Model

GCSE
DENSITY

Density is a measure of the amount of stuff within a given space, more specifically the amount of mass.

$$\rho = m/V$$

1. Write down the equation using words rather than symbols.

2. Name the units that each of the three variables in the equation are measured in.

3. Calculate the density (in kg/m³) of:

    a. A 690 kg object with a volume of 3.0 m³

    b. A 270 kg mass with a volume of 0.090 m³

    c. A 7.8 kg mass with a volume of 480 cm³

4. Rearrange the original equation to make **m** the subject, then ii) rearrange to make **V** the subject.

    i)   ii)

5. Fill in the table with the missing values (to 2 sf).

Density (kg/m³)	Mass (kg)	Volume (m³)	Calculations
	35.0	1.4	
	920	0.60	
1000	10		
8900	530		
1720		0.0093	
2300		200	

physics online

gcsephysicsonline.com/**density**

6. A swimming pool measures 25 m in length, 8.0 m in width and 1.2 m in depth.

    a. Calculate the volume of the swimming pool

Water has a density of ρ_{water} = 1000 kg/m³.

    b. Calculate the mass of water inside the swimming pool

A heavy brick is often used for training purposes in the pool. A brick has dimensions of approximately 18 cm in length, 9.0 cm in height and 8.0 cm in depth and a density 1.9 times that of water.

    c. Calculate the mass of the brick

7. A box of cornflakes has a mass of 900 g and has side lengths of 40 cm, 25 cm and 10 cm.

    Calculate the average density in kg/m³ of the cornflakes

8. Palladium has a density of approximately ρ = 12 g/cm³.

    a. Calculate the volume in cm³ that 3.6 kg of palladium would take up

Palladium sells for £51 per gram.

    b. Calculate the dimensions of a cube of palladium that costs £800 000

GCSE
SPECIFIC HEAT CAPACITY 1

The specific heat capacity (shc) of a substance is the energy absorbed or released in order to raise or lower the temperature of 1 kg of that substance by 1 °C.

change in thermal energy = mass x specific heat capacity x change in temperature

1. Name the units that each of the four variables in the equation are measured in.

2. Write down the equation using symbols rather than words.

3. Calculate the change in thermal energy of:

    a. A 4.0 kg mass with a specific heat capacity of 238 J/kg°C that has its temperature raised by 13 °C

    b. A 0.30 kg mass with a specific heat capacity of 23 J/kg°C that has its temperature raised by 127 °C

4. i) Rearrange the equation to make **m** the subject, ii) rearrange to make **c** the subject and iii) rearrange to make **Δθ** the subject.

    i)   ii)   iii)

5. Fill in the table with the missing values (to 2 sf).

ΔE (J)	m (kg)	c (J/kg°C)	Δθ (°C)	Calculations
	3.2	4200	5.0	
	12	2100	7.1	
4700	3.9		6.0	
1500	0.51		13	
820		1200	9.9	
28		230	32	
1700	0.026	1000		

6. A puddle of water has a mass of 5.0 kg and a temperature of 15 °C. In the evening, the puddle's temperature drops to 3.0 °C. c_{water} = 4200 J/kg°C

    a. Calculate the change in energy, if we assume no water is lost to evaporation

A student claims that if the temperature were to drop by half the amount, the change in energy would also be half.

    b. Use calculations to back up the student's claim

It rains overnight, causing the mass of the puddle to increase. The next evening, the puddle's temperature drops from 15 °C to 3.0 °C but the change in energy is 30% greater than in part a.

    c. Calculate the mass of the water puddle

7. A scientist spills 0.72 kg of liquid mercury onto the floor. Whilst the scientist goes to get equipment to clean it up, the liquid warms by 3.0 °C. $c_{mercury}$ = 126 J/kg°C

    a. Calculate the change in energy

The scientist wants to compare an unknown liquid to mercury. They pour 0.72 kg of the new liquid on the floor. Its change in energy is the same as the mercury in part a. but its temperature rises by 6.3 °C.

    b. Calculate the unknown liquid's specific heat capacity

8. Aluminium has a specific heat capacity 900 J/kg°C and a density of 2.7g/cm³.

280 g of aluminium is heated from an initial temperature of 15°C so that it absorbs 3820 J of energy.

Calculate its final temperature

The equation for the change in energy of an object involving the specific heat capacity can be written using symbols as:

$$\Delta E = mc\Delta\theta$$

1. A kettle can heat a maximum of 1.5 kg of water to boiling. A scientist fills the kettle up fully with water at 15 °C. c_{water} = 4.2 kJ/kg°C

   a. Calculate the energy needed to boil the kettle of water (assuming it is 100% efficient)

   The scientist wants to use 20% less energy when boiling the kettle. They decide to boil less water, again starting at 15 °C.

   b. Calculate the mass of water needed to transfer 20% less energy

   The scientist hears that milk has a specific heat capacity of 3.93 kJ/kg°C.

   c. Calculate how much energy it would take to raise 2 pints of milk to 100 °C if it was initially in a fridge at 4.0 °C (1 pint = 568 ml and the density of milk is similar to water)

2. A 0.70 kg block of copper is heated using a 150 W heater. In one and a half minutes, the copper block's temperature has been raised from 12 °C to 63 °C.

   Calculate the specific heat capacity of copper.

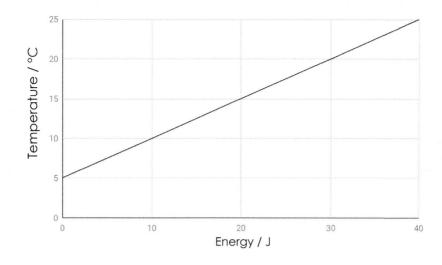

3. The graph above shows how the energy supplied to a massive 4.0 g diamond changes its temperature. The diamond starts at 5.0 °C and is carefully supplied with a total of 40 J of energy.

    a. Calculate the specific heat capacity of diamond

    b. Describe how the graph would look if a 6.0 g diamond was tested, again starting at 5.0 °C and supplied with 40 J of energy

4. Lithium has one of the highest specific heat capacities of any metal. A large 2300 g block of lithium is heated from 20 °C, such that it absorbs 503 kJ. $c_{lithium} = 3560 J/kg°C$

    a. Calculate the lithium block's final temperature

    b. If the same amount of energy had been transferred to the same mass of water at 20 °C, calculate final temperature of the water and compare this to the value for lithium

GCSE
SPECIFIC LATENT HEAT

The specific latent heat of a substance is the energy released or absorbed in order to change the state of 1 kg of that substance without changing the temperature.

energy required for a change of state = mass x specific latent heat

1. Name the units that each of the three variables in the equation are measured in.

2. Write down the equation using symbols rather than words.

3. Calculate the energy needed to change the state of the following.

   L_{water} (solid to liquid) = 334 kJ/kg L_{water} (liquid to gas) = 2260 kJ/kg.

   a. 2.1 kg of water into water vapour

   b. 350 g of ice into water

4. i) Rearrange the equation to make **m** the subject then ii) rearrange to make **L** the subject.

   i)   ii)

5. Fill in the table with the missing values (to 2 sf).

E (J)	m (kg)	L (J/kg)	Calculations
	3.4	340 000	
	59	210 000	
25 000	0.011		
8 900	0.040		
59 000		200 000	
42 000		460 000	

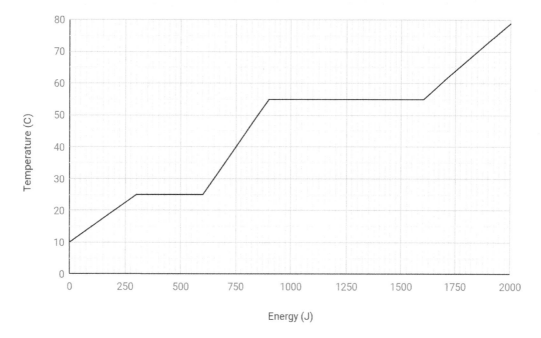

6. The graph shows what happens to the temperature of an unknown substance when energy is supplied. The substance has a mass of 2.5 kg.

   a. From the graph, calculate the substance's specific latent heat of fusion (solid to liquid) and vaporisation (liquid to gas)

   The mass of the substance is changed such that 40% more energy is needed to change it from a solid to a liquid.

   b. Calculate the new mass of the substance

7. Water has different values of specific latent heat for different transitions:

$L_{(solid\ to\ liquid)}$	= 334 kJ/kg
$L_{(liquid\ to\ gas)}$	= 2260 kJ/kg
C_{water}	= 4200 J/kg°C

   Calculate how much thermal energy is required to fully change 370g of ice at 0°C into water vapour.

Atomic Structure

GCSE
ATOMS AND ISOTOPES

Atoms make up everything you see around you. Atomic elements are defined by their number of protons whereas isotopes of elements have a different number of neutrons.

1. Write down the relative charges of the proton, electron and neutron.

2. Write down where the majority of an atom's mass is and what particles it contains.

3. Write down where you would find the electrons in an atom.

4. Describe what happens when an electron in an atom a) loses energy and b) gains energy.

    a.

    b.

5. Explain the role electrons in the outer shell have in the behaviour of an element (GCSE Chemistry style question).

6. Define the atomic number of an element.

7. Define the mass number of an element.

8. Write down how we use the symbols of a chemical element, and its mass and atomic numbers to represent elements.

9. Elements are neutrally charged. Write down what this tells us about the numbers of electrons, protons and neutrons within the atom.

gcsephysicsonline.com/**atoms**

10. Write down the definition of an 'isotope'.

11. The number of protons, electrons and neutrons in an atom is always a whole number (an integer). Explain why an element's mass number is not always a whole number on the periodic table.

12. Describe how you would work out the number of neutrons in an element if you know its atomic and mass numbers.

13. Define the term 'ion'.

14. Describe J.J. Thomson's plum pudding model.

15. Explain the results of the alpha-scattering experiment and what this proves about the structure of the atom.

GCSE
RADIOACTIVE DECAY

Unstable nuclei emit either particles or electromagnetic
radiation to become more stable. This is called radioactive decay.

1. Name the three most common types of radiation, and their symbols, that are
    released when a nucleus decays.

2. Write down i) what an alpha particle is made of and ii) what a beta particle is made
    of.

    i)   ii)

3. Fill in the table.

Type of radiation	Alpha (α)		Gamma (γ)
Charge		-1	neutral
Relative mass	4		
Object that stops the radiation			
Does the radiation change the element?			

4. Define the atomic number of an element and write down its symbol.

5. Define the mass number of an element and write down its symbol.

6. Write down what happens to an element's atomic number if it undergoes i) alpha
    emission, ii) beta emission and iii) gamma emission.

    i)   ii)   iii)

7. Write down what happens to an element's mass number if it undergoes i) alpha
    emission, ii) beta emission and iii) gamma emission.

    i)   ii)   iii)

8. Describe the process that allows beta decay to take place. Think about how a
    negatively charged particle can be emitted from a nucleus that only contains
    positive and neutral particles (protons and neutrons).

physics
online

gcsephysicsonline.com/**radiation**

9. Fill in the boxes to complete the general nuclear equation describing alpha emission for an element, X, decaying into element Y.

$$^{A}_{Z}X \rightarrow {}^{A-\square}_{Z-\square}Y + {}^{\square}_{\square}\square$$

10. Complete the nuclear equation for radon undergoing alpha decay.

$$^{226}Ra \rightarrow {}_{86}Rn +$$

11. Fill in the boxes to complete the general nuclear equation describing beta emission for an element, X, decaying into element Z.

$$^{\square}_{\square}X \rightarrow {}_{Z\square 1}Z + {}^{\square}_{\square}\square$$

12. Complete the nuclear equation for carbon undergoing beta decay.

$$_{6}C \rightarrow {}^{14}N +$$

13. Write down the general nuclear equation for an element, X, undergoing gamma decay.

$$^{A}_{Z}X \rightarrow$$

14. Write down the nuclear equation for cobalt-60 undergoing gamma decay. Cobalt has an atomic number, Z = 27.

15. Write down if the following decays are possible and if they are, name the process of decay (you may need a periodic table to help you).

    a. Thorium-232 can decay to radium-228

    b. Carbon-14 can decay into oxygen-14

    c. Uranium-238 can decay to thorium-232

    d. Technetium-99 can decay into technetium-99

    e. Lithium-8 can decay into beryllium-8

GCSE
HALF-LIFE

A sample of radioactive nuclei will decay exponentially. This means that the number of nuclei of the original element will decrease by the same proportion for each time period of the same length. The time for a sample to halve is its half-life.

1. Write down the unit for activity.

2. Define the half-life of an element in terms of its activity.

3. State if the following are examples of exponential decay:

    a. The number of original nuclei of an element halves after 10 s, halves again after another 10 s and halves again after another 10 s

    b. The activity of an element halves after 10 s, halves again after another 20 s and halves again after another 30 s

    c. The activity of an element reduces by a third after one minute, reduces by a third again after another minute and reduces by a third again after another minute

4. Complete the following:

    a. After 1 half-life, the activity is $\frac{1}{2}$ the original value

    b. After __2__ half-lives, the activity 1/4 the original value

    c. After __4__ half-lives, the activity 1/16 the original value

    d. After 5 half-lives, the activity is _____ the original value

5. A sample of an element has an initial activity of 3.00×10^{11} Bq. Calculate the activity after:

    a. One half-life

    b. Three half-lives

6. Nobelium-259 has a half-life of 58 minutes. A sample is measured as having an initial activity of 8.00×10^8 Bq.

    a. Calculate the estimated activity of the sample after three half-lives

    b. Calculate the estimated activity of the sample after 4 hours and 50 minutes

After some time has passed, the activity of the sample is measured at 6.25×10^6 Bq.

    c. Calculate how much time has passed since the original measurement

7. Carbon-14 is a radioactive isotope that has a half-life of 5730 years and is used in carbon dating. The remains of an archaeological specimen is tested, a sample containing carbon-14 is estimated to have an activity that is 3.125 % of its original value.

    Calculate the approximate age of the bones.

8. A sample of fermium-253 has an initial activity of 6.4×10^{10} Bq. After 12 days, the activity falls to 4.0×10^9 Bq.

    a. Calculate the half-life of fermium-253

    b. Calculate the estimated activity of the sample 3 weeks after the initial measurement

GCSE
FISSION AND FUSION

Fission occurs when a heavy nucleus splits
whereas fusion occurs when two light nuclei join together.

1. Write down two types of heavy isotopes that are commonly used in nuclear reactors for nuclear **fission**.

2. Write down the name given to the two smaller nuclei that are produced from fission.

3. Write down what else is released from nuclear fission.

4. Describe how the fission of one nucleus can lead to a chain reaction and potentially an explosion.

5. Write down the famous equation that describes the amount of energy released from the nucleus in a nuclear reaction.

6. Briefly describe how electricity is produced by a nuclear power station, starting with the fission of radioactive nuclei.

7. Describe how the rate of reaction in a nuclear power station can be increased or decreased.

physics online

gcsephysicsonline.com/**fission-and-fusion**

8. Explain the problems spent fuel rods present to the environment.

9. Describe some benefits of nuclear fission compared to fossil fuel power stations.

10. Write down where in the Universe you would find nuclear **fusion** occurring naturally.

11. Write down the particle(s) within a hydrogen nucleus.

12. Write down the particle(s) within a helium nucleus.

13. Two hydrogen nuclei can fuse together, forming a deuterium nucleus. However, deuterium nuclei contain one proton and one neutron, so explain what must have happened in this reaction.

14. A deuterium nucleus fuses together with another hydrogen nucleus (none of the protons or neutrons change in this reaction). Write down the number of protons and neutrons in the resulting particle and the element it is an isotope of.

15. The particle in question 14 can fuse with another of the same particle to produce a helium nucleus with two protons and two neutrons. Write down the particles that must be ejected when this occurs.

16. Write down the problems scientists currently face making nuclear fusion a viable energy source on Earth.

Forces and Motion

GCSE
IDENTIFYING FORCES

Force is a vector quantity, meaning that it has size and direction.
There are many different forces that exist in the world around us.

1. Write down the unit that force is measured in.

2. Explain the difference between contact and non-contact forces.

3. Give some examples of a) contact forces and b) non-contact forces.

    a.

    b.

4. Many people use the terms mass and weight to mean the same thing, when in fact the mass and weight of an object are different.

    a. Define the meaning of weight

    b. Describe the differences between mass and weight

    c. Write down the formula for weight in both symbols and words

    d. Write down the value of the gravitational field strength on (or very near to) the surface of Earth

5. Explain how friction is caused.

6. Explain why seemingly smooth surfaces still cause friction.

7. Describe how a lubricant reduces friction between two surfaces.

8. Explain how a fluid produces drag on a solid object.

9. Identify the forces acting on the following objects:

   a. A motorbiker riding along the road at a steady speed

   b. A swimmer floating in the sea

   c. A rugby ball that is at the highest point in its flight path after it has been kicked (moving to the right)

GCSE
FREE BODY DIAGRAMS

Free body, or force, diagrams, are a simple way of displaying the forces acting on an object.

1. Name the four main forces acting on a car, travelling at constant velocity.

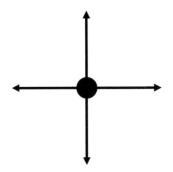

On the left is a force diagram of the car in question 1.

a. Describe what the black dot represents

b. Match each of the four forces to an arrow

2. Describe the resultant force acting on an object if it is at rest or travelling at a constant velocity.

3. Describe the resultant force acting on an object that is accelerating or decelerating.

4. If two forces are acting on an object in the same direction, describe how we could display this on a force diagram.

5. Explain how we display the size of the forces acting on an object on a free body diagram.

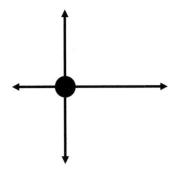

6. The force diagram on the left shows the forces acting on a different car moving from left to right.

a. Describe the motion of the car

The driver of the car (on the previous page) puts the car in neutral and slams on the brakes, i.e. there is no forward force.

b. Draw a diagram showing the forces acting on the car, a second after braking.

7. a. Draw a free body diagram showing the forces acting on a homemade rocket a split second after taking off. There is a slight wind blowing from left to right.

b. Draw a free body diagram showing the forces acting on the same rocket after some time has passed and is decelerating i.e. the upward forces are less than the downward forces. The wind blowing from left to right has increased.

8. a. Draw a free body diagram showing the forces acting on a monkey that is hanging from a branch by its tail.

b. Describe how the diagram would differ if it showed the monkey leaping midway between two trees and explain what this tells you about the motion of the monkey.

GCSE
RESOLVING FORCES

The force acting on an object at an angle can be resolved into two or more components, usually the horizontal and vertical components. Forces can be resolved either mathematically or graphically (by scale drawing).

1. Write down Pythagoras's theorem for right angled triangles.

2. Write down the three trigonometric identities that are in SOH-CAH-TOA.

3. If a force acts on an object at an angle, it can be resolved into horizontal and vertical components. For the following four questions, resolve the force into its two components.

   a. Resolve a single force of 6.0 N acting at 45° to the horizontal.

   b. Resolve a single force of 4.6 N acting at 35° to the horizontal.

c. Resolve a single force of 3.7 N acting at 70° to the horizontal.

4. A horizontal force of 4.3 N to the right and a vertical force of 3.2 N up act on an object. Find the resultant force acting on the object.

5. An explorer pulls a sled behind her by a rope that ties around her waist. She pulls the sled with a force of 230 N at an angle of 43.8° above the ground.

   Resolve the tension in the rope using a mathematical method.

GCSE
WORK DONE

Mechanical work done is the name we give to the energy transferred by a force to move an object with mass a certain distance.

work done = force x distance

1. Write down the equation using symbols rather than words and name the units that each of the three variables in the equation are measured in.

2. Explain the relationship between the direction of the force and the distance travelled.

3. Calculate the work done by:

    a. A 25 N force acting over a distance of 6.0 m

    b. A 0.45 N force acting over a distance of 10 cm

    c. A 100 kN force acting over 5.3 km

4. i) Rearrange the original equation to make **F** the subject, then ii) make **s** the subject.

    i)   ii)

5. Fill in the table with the missing values.

Work done (J)	Force (N)	Distance (m)	Calculations
	912	890	
87	52		
7900	0.70		
670		17.0	
90		12	

6. A school janitor pulls his cart full of cleaning supplies along with a constant force of 89 N against friction.

    a. Calculate the work done by the janitor as he pulls the cart along a 28 m hallway

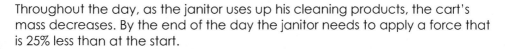

    Throughout the day, as the janitor uses up his cleaning products, the cart's mass decreases. By the end of the day the janitor needs to apply a force that is 25% less than at the start.

    b. Calculate the work done by the janitor as he pulls the cart at the end of the day along the same hallway

The janitor uses a mop bucket to clean up some mess. He drags the mop with a force of 17 N across the floor.

    c. Calculate the distance, in the direction of the force, covered by the mop head as he does 850 J of work

7. A lift in a hospital, which itself has a mass of 250 kg, has a maximum capacity of 700 kg. Some doctors and nurses get in the lift such that the lift is at 80% capacity.

    a. Calculate the work done by the lift as it carries the medical staff up 3 floors (each floor is 2.4 m high)

The lift is used to transport a heavy piece of medical equipment, that has a mass of 540 kg, to a higher floor by two hospital workers that have an average mass of 80 kg. The work done by the lift is 111 720 J.

    b. Calculate how many floors up the lift carries the workers and the equipment

GCSE
SPRINGS

Springs store elastic potential energy if they are either extended or compressed. How much a spring is extended or compressed, by a certain force, is dependent on its spring constant.

F = ke   (it can also be written as **F = kx** or **F = kΔl**)

1. Write down the equation using words rather than symbols and name the units that each of the three variables in the equation are measured in.

2. Define the extension of a spring.

3. Calculate the force acting on a spring with:

    a. A spring constant of 80 N/m that is extended by 0.25 m

    b. A spring constant of 0.50 N/m that is extended by 700 mm

4. i) Rearrange the equation to make **k** the subject, then ii) rearrange to make **e** the subject.

    i)   ii)

5. Fill in the table with the missing values.

Force (N)	Spring constant (N/m)	Extension (m)	Calculations
	0.40	0.90	
	18	0.36	
12		0.60	
25		0.050	
1.0	7.4		
8.5	90		

6. Write down how you would describe the behaviour of a material that has been;

    a. stretched beyond the limit of proportionality, so that it cannot return to its original shape

    b. stretched within the limit of proportionality, so that it returns to its original shape

7. State Hooke's Law.

8. A 7.0 cm long stretchy spring has a spring constant of approximately 16 N/m.

    a. Calculate the **total** length of the spring if a force of 5.4 N acts to stretch it

The spring is hung on a hook and a mass is hung on the bottom.

    b. Calculate the mass needed to extend the band by 1.2 cm

9. A student wants to test the properties of a spring they found. They hang a mass on the spring and measure the results, which are in the table below.

    a. Complete the table below on the left by calculating the force applied on the spring by the mass (use g = 10 N/kg) and plot your results on the axes on the right

Mass (kg)	Extension (m)	Force (N)
0	0	
0.4	0.006	
0.8	0.012	
1.2	0.017	
1.6	0.024	
2.0	0.031	
2.4	0.036	

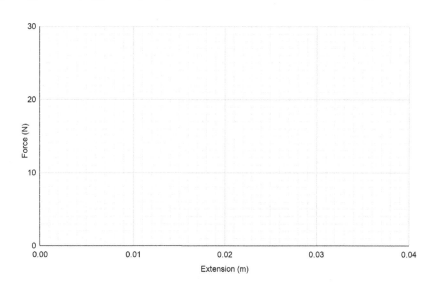

    b. Calculate the gradient of the graph and explain what this represents

GCSE
MOMENTS

A moment is the turning effect caused by applying a force at a distance from the pivot point (or turning point).

moment = force x distance

1. Name the units that each of the three variables in the equation are measured in.

2. Describe the relationship between the direction of the force and the distance to the turning point.

3. Calculate the moment of:

   a. A 45 N force acting at a perpendicular distance of 4.0 m

   b. A 9.0 N force acting at a perpendicular distance of 70 cm

4. i) Rearrange the equation to make **force** the subject, then ii) rearrange to make **distance** the subject.

   i)   ii)

5. Fill in the table with the missing values.

Moment (Nm)	Force (N)	Distance (m)	Calculations
	0.40	20	
	780	0.250	
52.2	90.0		
800	160		
1.4		0.050	
270		6.50	

6. Some students go to visit a museum. One of the exhibits is an incredibly heavy door with several door handles attached at different points. A worker explains that a force of 2.10 kN at a perpendicular distance of 1.50 m from the hinges is needed to open the door.

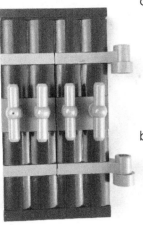

a. Explain why a normal door has a handle that is placed at the edge, on the opposite side to the hinges

b. Calculate the moment needed to open the museum door

None of the students can open the door on their own but the two strongest, Celine and Noah, can pull the door if they work together. Noah pulls on one handle with a force of 1.20 kN at a perpendicular distance of 1.40 m.

c. Calculate the moment produced by Noah

Celine pulls with a force of 1.40 kN.

d. Calculate the perpendicular distance from the hinges to the handle Celine is pulling on

Four other students try pulling on the door. Beth pulls with a force of 900 N at a distance of 60.0 cm, Nicole pulls with a force of 1.20 kN at a distance of 80.0 cm, Rachel pulls with a force of 800 N at a distance of 30.0 cm and Yasmine pulls with an unknown force at a distance of 1.25 m.

e. Calculate the force that Yasmine applies on her handle if they just manage to open the door

GCSE
PRESSURE AT A SURFACE

The pressure acting on the surface of a solid is the force applied per unit area.

pressure = force/area

1. Write down the equation using symbols rather than words and name the units that each of the three variables in the equation are measured in, including two different units for pressure.

2. Write down the approximate value of atmospheric pressure on Earth at sea level.

3. Calculate the pressure caused by:

    a. A 120 N force acting over an area of 1.2 m^2

    b. A 380 N force acting over an area of 0.250 m^2

    c. A 1.7 kN force acting over 0.0017 m^2

4. i) Rearrange the original equation to make **F** the subject, then ii) rearrange to make **A** the subject.

    i)   ii)

5. Fill in the table with the missing values.

Pressure (Pa)	Force (N)	Area (m^2)	Calculations
	12.0	200	
101 000	101 000		
43 000	86 000		
22.8		0.00500	
700		68.0	

6. The atmospheric pressure at sea-level on Earth is 101 kPa. Because everything around us is at the same pressure we don't notice it. The surface area of a human varies between approximately 0.25 m² for a newborn baby to 1.8 m² for the average adult.

   a. Calculate the force from the atmosphere acting on a newborn baby

   b. Calculate the force from the atmosphere acting on an average adult

The force acting on a football pitch due to air pressure is 707 MN. The pitch is 100 m long.

   c. Calculate the area of a football pitch and its width

7. A science lab wants to test the strength of a sheet of metal to see how it deforms. A sample is cut out and suspended by its four corners. **Ignore** the effect of air pressure in your calculations.

   A square weight, with mass 110 kg and sides of 10 cm, is placed on the metal sheet.

   a. Calculate the pressure caused by the weight on the metal

The metal does not bend so a different weight is used. A rectangular block, with a mass of 150 kg, is placed on the metal. The surface in contact with the sheet measures 20 cm x 5.0 cm.

   b. Calculate the pressure caused by this weight on the metal

Still the metal does not bend. The scientists balance a small metal cone of mass 18 kg whose pointed end bends the metal sheet, leaving behind an indentation.

   c. Without using calculations, explain why the cone is able to bend the sheet even though the mass is much smaller

GCSE
PRESSURE AT A DEPTH IN FLUIDS

The pressure acting on an object submerged in a fluid is dependent on the height of fluid above it, the density of the fluid and the gravitational field strength.

pressure = height of fluid x density of fluid x gravitational field strength

1. Write down the equation using symbols rather than words and name the units that each of the four variables in the equation are measured in, including two different units for pressure.

2. Calculate the increase in pressure (from atmospheric pressure) at a depth of:

   a. 2.9 m deep in a pool of water (ρ_{water} = 1000 kg/m³)

   b. 8.0 km under the ocean's surface ($\rho_{deep\ ocean}$ = 1060 kg/m³)

   c. 30 cm deep in a tank of liquid mercury ($\rho_{mercury}$ = 13 700 kg/m³)

3. Rearrange the equation to make i) **h** the subject, ii) **ρ** the subject and iii) **g** the subject

   i)   ii)   iii)

4. Fill in the table with the missing values. (g = gravitational field strength.)

Pressure (kPa)	Height (m)	g (N/kg)	Density (kg/m³)	Calculations
101	3.40	9.80		
700	90.0	6.80		
101		9.80	1000	
150		9.80	800	
101	10.2		1320	
5.30	3.10		909	

5. An Olympic diver diving off a 10 m high platform into a pool can go as deep as 3.5 m.

   a. Calculate the **increase** in pressure acting on the diver at this depth

   ρ_{water} = 1000 kg/m³

   b. Calculate the depth at which the **total** pressure acting on the diver is 150 kPa

   In an alternate reality, diving competitions are held on the moon in an artificial atmosphere that is at the same pressure as Earth's atmosphere. The gravitational field strength on the moon is about 1/6 of the value as Earth's gravitational field strength.

   c. Calculate the increase in pressure acting on a diver underwater at a depth of 2.0 m

6. A deep-sea diver trains in a deep freshwater tank. They need to be able to withstand a **total** pressure that is 2.5 times that of atmospheric pressure.

   Calculate how deep they would need to dive to experience this.

7. The method of calculating pressure in fluids can be applied to calculate an approximate value of atmospheric pressure as well. After all, air is a fluid.

   a. Write down the value of atmospheric pressure at sea-level

   The atmosphere is estimated to be approximately 100 km high.

   b. Calculate the **average** density of the atmosphere, assuming that **g** is constant (please note that the average density is much less dense than the density at sea-level and that g is slightly weaker 100 km above the surface)

GCSE
SPEED

Speed is a measure of how quickly an object is travelling.

$$v = s/t$$

1. Write down the equation using words rather than symbols and name the units that each of the three variables in the equation are measured In.

2. Calculate the speed of an object that travels:

    a. 500 m in 10 s

    b. 9.0 km in one minute

    c. 0.80 cm in 4.0 s

3. Write down or calculate:

    a. How many seconds are in one hour

    b. How fast 1.0 m/s is in miles per hour (1 mile ≈ 1600 m)

4. i) Rearrange the equation to make **s** the subject, then ii) rearrange to make **t** the subject.

    i)   ii)

5. Fill in the table with the missing values.

Speed (m/s)	Distance (m)	Time (s)	Calculations
10		900	
3.00		3600	
0.89	890		
12	852		

6. Average speed cameras are used to enforce different speed limit zones on the motorway. A car takes exactly 15 minutes to cover 18 miles in a 70 mph zone.

    a. Calculate if the car is breaking the speed limit

A different car takes 2 minute and 45 seconds to travel 4.2 km in a 60 mph zone.

    b. Calculate if this car is breaking the speed limit (60 mph ≈ 27 m/s)

A lorry is limited to a top speed of 90 km/h.

    c. Calculate its top speed in m/s

The same lorry enters a 60 mph zone that is 4.6 miles long. The driver wants to know how long it will take him to travel the length of the 60 mph zone.

    d. Calculate how much time the lorry would take to travel the 4.6 miles

The lorry is 22.5m long. The driver thinks to himself that it would take him a quarter of an hour, travelling at max speed, to cover a thousand lorry-lengths.

    e. Calculate whether or not the driver is correct

GCSE
VELOCITY

Velocity is the speed of an object in a given direction.

$$v = s/t$$

1. Write down the equation for velocity using words rather than symbols and name the units that each of the three variables in the equation are measured in.

2. Speed and distance are examples of which type of quantity:

3. Velocity and displacement are examples of:

4. Describe the difference between distance and displacement.

5. Describe the difference between speed and velocity.

6. Calculate the average velocity of:

    a. A car that is displaced 640 m in 40 s

    b. A tennis ball that is displaced 12 m in 0.80 s

    c. A toy train that travels 80cm forwards then 30cm backwards in 10 s

    d. An Olympic swimmer who swims 100 m in a 50 m pool in 48 s

7. A wildlife photographer sets out to find some crocodiles. She drives her 4x4 for 45 minutes on a perfectly straight road and covers 35 miles (1 mile ≈ 1600 m).

   a. Calculate the explorer's velocity in m/s

The photographer sees some crocodiles in a lake. The crocodiles' swimming speed is measured at 4.0 m/s.

   b. Calculate how long a crocodile would take to cross the 48 m wide lake if it swam directly from shore to shore

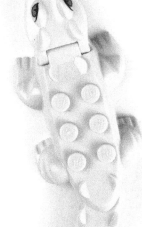

A crocodile swims at a constant speed of 4.0 m/s from shore to shore but takes 24 s to do so.

   c. Explain how this can be the case and include a calculation for the velocity of the crocodile

One crocodile starts to chase the photographer on land! She zig-zags as she runs so that the crocodile has to zig-zag as well, slowing it down. Her car is 80 m away but they cover a distance of 240 m.

   d. Calculate the ratio between the explorer's speed and their velocity

The photographer drives straight home in a panic and gets into bed.

   e. Calculate the average velocity of the photographer from the moment she wakes up in bed in the morning to when she gets back into bed in the evening

8. The Earth travels around the Sun in a circular orbit with a radius of approximately 1.5×10^{11} m. As we know, the Earth takes 365.25 days to complete an orbit.

   Calculate the average velocity of the Earth as it completes exactly half an orbit.

GCSE
ACCELERATION

Acceleration is the rate of change of an object's velocity with respect to time.
In other words, it is a measure of how quickly the velocity of an object changes.

acceleration = change in velocity/time

1. Name the units that each of the variables in the equation are measured in.

2. Write down the equation using symbols rather than words.

3. Calculate the acceleration of:

    a. An object going from rest to 14 m/s in 10 s

    b. An object decelerating from 100 m/s to 5.0 m/s in 38s

    c. An object accelerating from rest to 120 m/s in one and a half minutes

4. i) Rearrange the equation to make **v** the subject, ii) rearrange to make **u** the subject and iii) rearrange to make **t** the subject.

    i)   ii)   iii)

5. Fill in the table with the missing values.

a (m/s²)	v (m/s)	u (m/s)	t (s)	Calculations
3.0		5.0	45.0	
24.0		12.8	3.00	
11.1	66.9		2.00	
10	136		12	
135	36.5	23.0		
1.4	423.3	3.5		

physics
online

gcsephysicsonline.com/**acceleration**

6. Ironman decides to test how fast he can accelerate vertically upwards. He starts from the ground, at rest, and gets to a velocity of 230 m/s in 12 s.

   a. Calculate Ironman's acceleration

   b. If Ironman were to change direction, whilst travelling at a constant 230 m/s, explain whether he would be accelerating or not

After making some adjustments, Ironman repeats his test. This time, he gets to a velocity of 260 m/s but it takes him 14 s.

   c. Determine if Ironman's acceleration has improved

7. A teacher attaches a gas cylinder to a wheelie bin. She opens the cylinder, releasing the gas, which accelerates the bin at a constant rate of 1.2 m/s^2. The bin reaches a final velocity of 23 m/s.

   a. Calculate the time the bin takes to accelerate to 23 m/s

She wants to increase the bin's final velocity. She pushes the bin so that it's travelling at an initial velocity of 3.6 m/s. The acceleration is still 1.2 m/s^2.

   b. Calculate the final velocity after 20 s

Still unhappy with the bin's final velocity, she tweaks the gas cylinder such that the acceleration is increased to 1.5 m/s^2. However, this means the cylinder can only accelerate the bin for 15 s. She pushes the bin at an initial velocity of 4.7 m/s.

   c. Calculate if the bin reaches a final velocity greater than in part b.

   d. Calculate how fast the bin would have to be initially travelling for the bin to reach 30 m/s in 15 s

GCSE
DISTANCE-TIME GRAPHS

Distance-time graphs show us how far an object travels within a certain time. They can also be used to work out the speed of an object.

1. Write down the units for speed and hence the equation for speed.

2. Below is a simple distance-time graph for an object. Calculate the following:

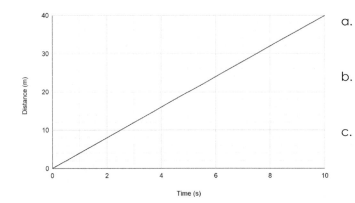

    a.   The distance travelled after 6 s

    b.   The time it takes to travel 36 m

    c.   The speed of the object

3. Below is a distance-time graph for a mountain-biker. Calculate the speed:

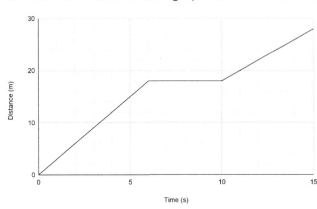

    a.   In the first 6 seconds

    b.   Between 6 and 10 seconds

    c.   Between 10 and 15 seconds

Using the graph, write down:

    d. The total distance covered

    e. The total time taken

    f. Hence, calculate the average speed of the mountain-biker

physics
online

gcsephysicsonline.com/**motion-graphs**

4. This is a distance-time graph showing the movements of a runaway robot.

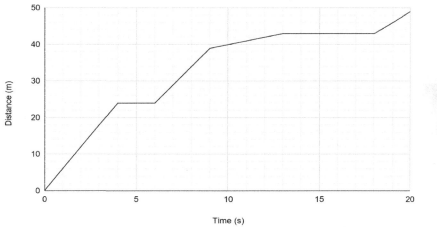 

a. Calculate the robot's maximum speed

b. Calculate the robot's minimum speed when moving

c. Calculate how long the robot was stationary for

d. Calculate the average speed of the robot **only when it is moving** i.e. not including the time the robot is stationary

5. Below is a distance-time graph of a dolphin swimming in the ocean.

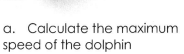

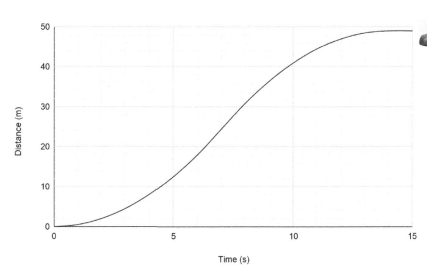

a. Calculate the maximum speed of the dolphin

b. Calculate the speed of the dolphin at 11 s

GCSE
VELOCITY-TIME GRAPHS

Velocity-time graphs show us an object's velocity over time. They can also be used to work out the acceleration and the total displacement of an object.

1. Write down the equations for acceleration and displacement.

2. State what the gradient and area under a velocity-time graph represent respectively.

3. Below is a velocity-time graph for a swordfish swimming in the ocean.

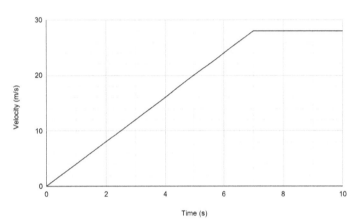

a.   Write down at which time the swordfish is stationary

b.   Write down the swordfish's velocity between 7 s and 10 s

c.   Calculate the swordfish's acceleration between 0 s and 7 s

d. Calculate the total displacement of the swordfish

Below is a different velocity-time graph for the same swordfish on a different swim.

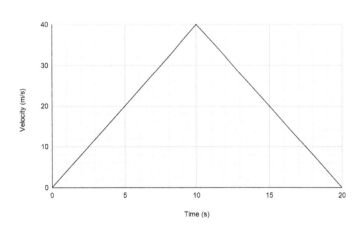

e.   Calculate the total displacement

f.   Calculate the average velocity

4. This is a velocity-time graph of an alien spaceship.

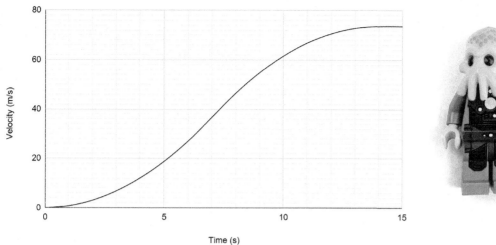

a. Calculate the average acceleration of the spaceship over 15 s

b. Calculate the maximum acceleration of the spaceship (steepest gradient)

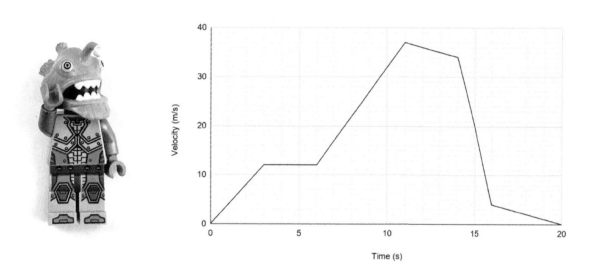

Above is a velocity-time graph for a different spaceship.

c. Determine the fastest velocity

d. Calculate which spaceship has a greater maximum **positive** acceleration

GCSE
EQUATIONS OF MOTION

The following worksheet is based on the relationship between the initial and final velocities of an object, its acceleration and the distance it travels.

final velocity² - initial velocity² = 2 x acceleration x distance

1. Name the units that each of the four variables in the equation are measured in.

2. Write down the equation using symbols rather than words.

3. i) Rearrange the equation to make **v** the subject, ii) rearrange to make **u** the subject, iii) rearrange to make **a** the subject and iv) rearrange to make **s** the subject.

    i)   ii)

    iii)   iv)

4. Fill in the table with the missing values (to 2 sf).

v (m/s)	u (m/s)	a (m/s²)	s (m)	Calculations
	0	12	56	
	5.0	2.5	67	
23		3.4	7.8	
12		10	3.9	
120	20		350	
79	0.10		47	
450	2.3	32		

5. A boxer goes for a run to improve her fitness. She starts at rest and slowly but constantly accelerates to a sprinting velocity of 7.0 m/s in a time of one and a half minutes.

   a. Calculate the boxer's acceleration

   b. Calculate the total distance travelled by the boxer

6. A dog escapes from its owner's front garden. The dog moves at an initial velocity of 3.0 m/s then accelerates at 1.4 m/s^2 over a distance of 58 m.

   a. Calculate the dog's final velocity

The dog reaches the speed calculated in part a. and runs out of energy. It immediately starts to slow down until it stops and lies down having travelled a further distance of 39 m.

   b. Calculate the dog's deceleration from maximum speed to rest

   c. Write down the total distance covered by the dog during its escape

The owner, travelling on their bike, accelerates from rest until they get to the position of the resting dog, reaching a final velocity of 10 m/s at this point.

   d. Calculate the owner's acceleration

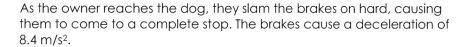

As the owner reaches the dog, they slam the brakes on hard, causing them to come to a complete stop. The brakes cause a deceleration of 8.4 m/s^2.

   e. Calculate the distance covered by the owner as they decelerate

GCSE
NEWTON'S SECOND LAW

The acceleration of an object is dependent on the force acting on it and its mass.

F = ma

1. Write down the equation in words rather than symbols and name the units that each of the three variables in the equation are measured in.

2. Write down a different equation for acceleration in terms of initial and final velocities.

3. Calculate the force acting on the following:

   a. A 20 kg mass being accelerated at 3.0 m/s^2

   b. A 0.70 kg mass being accelerated at 20 m/s^2

   c. A 60 g mass being accelerated at 20 km/s^2

   d. A 130 kg mass being accelerated from rest to 50 m/s in 25 s

4. Rearrange the first equation i) to make **m** the subject, then ii) to make **a** the subject.

   i)   ii)

5. Fill in the table with the missing values.

Force (N)	Mass (kg)	Acceleration (m/s^2)	Calculations
	80	0.25	
800	80		
800	20		
800		10	
1.00		1.098 x 10^{30}	

6. The average human has a mass of 75.0 kg.

    a. Calculate the weight of the average human (use g = 9.80 N/kg for this question)

The 'average' human jumps from a diving board into a swimming pool. Their weight provides the resultant force that accelerates them

    b. Ignoring air resistance, calculate their acceleration

A 3.50 g LEGO minifigure is dropped at exactly the same time. Calculate:

    c. The weight of the minifigure

    d. The resultant force of the minifigure

    e. The acceleration of the minifigure

    f. Compare you answers from part b. to part e.

7. A teenager has just passed their driving test. They borrow their mum's car to see how fast it will accelerate from 0 – 60 mph (equal to 27 m/s).

    a. It takes them 9.0 seconds. Calculate their acceleration

    b. The car has a mass of 1.2 tonnes. Calculate the average resultant force

They lose control at 60 mph and hit a lamp post causing the car to come to a complete stop in a time of 0.75 s.

    c. Calculate the deceleration of the car

GCSE
STOPPING DISTANCES

The distance it takes for a vehicle to come to a stop is dependent on both the reaction time of the driver (which affects the thinking distance) and the braking distance of the vehicle.

1. Define the stopping distance of a vehicle.

2. The stopping distance of a vehicle is the sum of two different distances.

    a. Name and describe one of the distances

    b. Name and describe the other distance

3. Write down four reasons why a driver's reaction time might be delayed.

4. As well as the driver's capacity to react, write down and explain something else that the thinking distance is dependent on.

5. Imagine a car is braking. Write down three things that might affect the braking distance.

6. Write down the equation for stopping distance in terms of the two distances given as answers in question 2.

7. Briefly describe an experiment to test the reaction time of a person.

8. Write down the equation for speed in terms of distance and time.

9. Hence write down the proportionality relationship between distance and speed while the driver reacts to put the brakes on (reaction time).

10. Write down the equation for the kinetic energy of the car travelling at velocity, v.

11. Describe the relationship between the initial kinetic energy of the car and the work done by the brakes on the wheels.

12. A student claims that stopping distance increases linearly with speed. Explain whether their claim is correct or not.

 **GCSE**
MOMENTUM

Momentum can be thought of as the quantity of motion that an object possesses. It is dependent on an object's mass and its velocity.

momentum = mass x velocity

1. Name the units that each of the three variables in the equation are measured in.

2. Write down the equation using symbols rather than words.

3. Calculate the momentum of:

    a. A 4.0 kg mass with a velocity of 8.0 m/s

    b. An 8.0 kg mass with a velocity of 4.0 m/s

    c. An 8.0 kg mass with a velocity of 8.0 m/s

4. i) Rearrange the equation to make **m** the subject and ii) rearrange to make **v** the subject.

    i)   ii)

5. Fill in the table with the missing values to 3 sf.

p (kg m/s)	m (kg)	v (m/s)	Calculations
	13.0	3.60	
	28.2	12.7	
340	67.0		
268	14.4		
80.0		128	
18.6		0.600	

6. A barbeque that has a mass of 32 kg is left outside during a hurricane. The strong wind causes the barbeque to travel at 0.90 m/s.

   a. Calculate the barbeque's momentum

The lid of the barbeque comes off and blows away. The lid has the same momentum as calculated in part a. but has a mass of 3.5 kg.

   b. Calculate the barbeque lid's velocity

7. A satellite has a mass of approximately 1.2 tonnes and travels at 7.0 km/s.

One tonne = 1000 kg

   a. Calculate the satellite's momentum

Because space is a vacuum, objects such as meteoroids can travel at very high velocities. A meteoroid with a mass of 120 kg has the same momentum as the satellite.

   b. Calculate the velocity of the meteoroid

   c. Display the ratio of the satellite's and the meteoroid's:

     i) masses

     ii) velocities

The meteoroid, which orbits the sun, has a constant speed, equal to the velocity calculated in part b.

   d. Explain why the momentum of the meteoroid is constantly changing

GCSE
CONSERVATION OF MOMENTUM

Momentum, like energy, is always conserved. In a closed system, the total sum of momentum before an event, like a collision, always equals the total sum of momentum after the event.

$$p_{before} = p_{after}$$

1. Write down the equation for the momentum of an object.

2. Complete the equation showing the relationship of two colliding objects with masses m_1 and m_2, initial velocities u_1 and u_2 and final velocities v_1 and v_2.

$$p_{1,before} + p_{2,before} = p_{1,after} + p_{2,after}$$

$$m_1 \_\_\_\_ + \_\_\_\_ u_2 = \_\_\_\_ \_\_\_\_ + m_2v_2$$

3. Calculate the total momentum of:

   a. A 2.0 kg mass and a 7.0 kg mass both travelling at 4.0 m/s in the same direction

   b. A 0.20 kg mass travelling at 120 m/s and an 80 kg mass travelling at 0.80 m/s in the same direction

   c. A 4.0 kg mass and a 3.0 kg mass both travelling at 8.0 m/s but in opposite directions

   d. A 5.0 kg mass travelling at 12 m/s travelling in one direction and a 20 kg mass travelling at 3.0 m/s in the opposite direction

4. Two sixth formers are playing rugby. One player has a mass of 70 kg and is travelling at 4.0 m/s. He collides with the other player (on his own team) who has a mass of 100 kg and is at rest.

   a. Calculate the total momentum of the two players

After the impact, the two students move off together.

   b. Calculate the final velocity of the two students

Later in the game, they collide again. This time the 100 kg student travels at 5.0 m/s and collides with the 70kg student who is at rest. After the collision, the 100 kg student stays at rest.

   c. Calculate the final velocity of the 70 kg student

5. Mary is surfing in Devon. She has a mass of 59 kg (including her board) and catches a wave which causes her to travel at a velocity of 5.5 m/s.

   a. Calculate Mary's momentum

A dolphin swims alongside Mary as they both travel at 6.8 m/s. The total combined momentum of the dolphin and Mary is 1140 kgm/s.

   b. Calculate the dolphin's mass

Mary catches a different wave. This wave propels her at 7.6 m/s but the dolphin swims directly at her at 5.1 m/s. The dolphin jumps out of the water and collides with Mary (luckily both are unhurt).

   c. Calculate the resulting velocity of both the dolphin and Mary if they 'stick' together after the collision

Light and Waves

GCSE
WAVE CALCULATIONS

The velocity (or speed) of a wave can be calculated by multiplying frequency by wavelength.

velocity = frequency x wavelength

1. Write down the equation using symbols rather than words.

2. Write down the equation describing the relationship between the frequency and the time period of a wave.

3. Calculate the velocity of:

    a. A wave with a wavelength of 12 m and a frequency of 3.0 Hz

    b. A wave with a wavelength of 0.10 m and a frequency of 120 Hz

    c. A wave with a wavelength of 1.0×10^{-6} m and a frequency of 3.0×10^{14} Hz

    d. Explain what type of wave travels at the same velocity as the wave in part c.

4. i) Rearrange the wave speed equation to make λ the subject, then ii) rearrange to make **f** the subject.

    i)   ii)

5. Fill in the table with the missing values.

Velocity (m/s)	Wavelength (m)	Frequency (Hz)	Calculations
	1.0×10^7	30	
3.0×10^8		4.7×10^{12}	
330		2.2×10^4	
3.0×10^8	1.2×10^{-6}		
14.2	499		

6. Batman is developing some sonar technology for his echolocation goggles. He stands in a cave holding a speaker and a timer 99.0 m away from the far end of the cave. Batman remembers that sound travels at about 330 m/s in air.

a. Calculate the time the sound waves take to travel to the far end and back

The sound wave completes 1,200 wave cycles in the time it takes to travel to the far end and back.

b. Calculate the time period of one wave cycle

c. Hence, calculate the frequency of the sound wave

d. Hence, calculate the wavelength of the sound wave to 2 sf

7. The Joker is developing some high-powered torches for his fight against Batman. He reads that the torch has a frequency of 5.30×10^{14} Hz and a wavelength of 5.66×10^{-7} m.

a. Show that the speed of light is about 3.00×10^8 m/s

The Joker claims that if he increases the frequency, then he could make the light travel faster.

b. Explain whether the Joker is correct or not

The Joker wants to produce light in the infrared zone at a wavelength, $\lambda = 950$ nm.

c. Calculate the frequency of this infrared light (1 nm = 1×10^{-9} m)

If a wave meets a boundary between two materials and cannot be transmitted through, it is either absorbed or bounced back into the material (medium) it has come from. This is reflection.

angle of incidence = angle of reflection

1. Explain what specular reflection means.

2. Explain what diffuse reflection means.

3. Give a reason why specular reflection can be more dangerous than diffuse reflection.

4. Draw a diagram of a beam of light reflecting off a plane mirror. Include labels for the normal, the angle of incidence, the angle of reflection and the mirror. Ensure you show the direction the light is travelling.

5. Complete the reflection diagram below and, using a protractor, measure the angle of incidence and the angle of reflection.

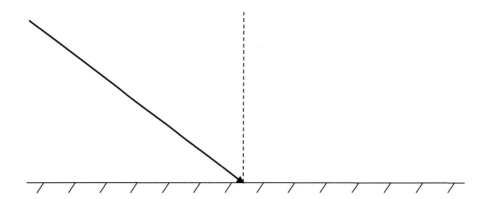

6. Complete the reflection diagram below and continue until the light escapes the mirrors.

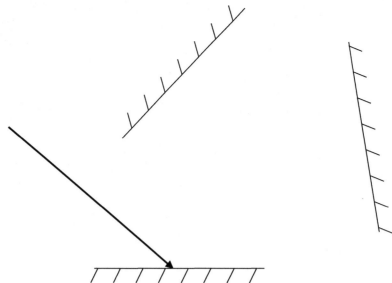

7. Complete the reflection diagrams below, label which is specular reflection and which is diffuse reflection.

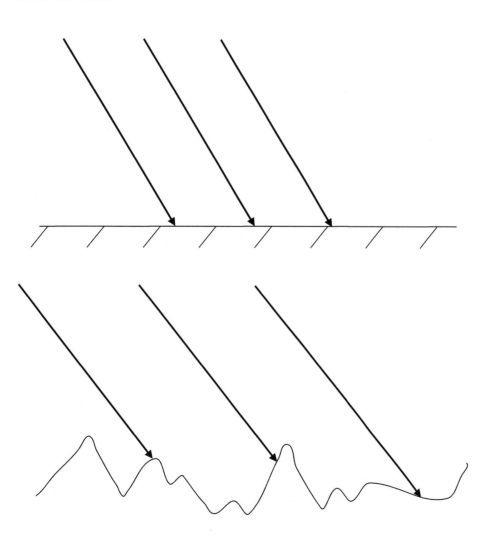

GCSE
ULTRASOUND SCANNING

Sound waves with a frequency above the range of human hearing are called ultrasound.

1. Write down the frequency limits for human hearing.

2. Explain why humans have an upper limit for the frequency of sound they can hear.

3. Describe some differences between sound waves and electromagnetic waves.

4. Write down the approximate speed of sound in air (at standard pressure and temperature).

5. Sound can also be used for echolocation. If we know the speed of sound and we measure the time it takes for the sound to be emitted, reflect off the object and return, we can calculate the distance.

   a. Write down the equation for speed, in terms of distance and time

   b. Rearrange the above equation for distance

   c. Explain why the above equation does **not** give the distance to an object using echolocation

6. Give an example and explain why it is useful for ultrasound to be only **partially** reflected.

7. Describe how the received ultrasound signal differs from the emitted signal.

8. Give an example where echolocation is used in nature.

9. Ultrasound is used for scanning pregnant women.

   a. Describe if there any risks posed by the use of ultrasound scanning

   b. Name some advantages of using ultrasound for pregnant women compared with other methods of seeing inside the body, such as X-rays for example

The frequency of ultrasound used in imaging is approximately 2.0 MHz.

   c. Assuming the speed it travels through tissue is 1600 m/s, calculate the wavelength of the ultrasound

The ultrasound source is placed on the skin of a pregnant woman during a scan so waves only travel tens of centimetres. This means they return very quickly. We assume the speed of sound is the same as in question c.

   d. Calculate the time that the ultrasound takes to be emitted, reflected off a boundary 20 cm from the scanner and received back

The ultrasound waves are not fully reflected, they are partly transmitted and partly reflected.

   e. Describe how the computer is able to build a picture of the baby using ultrasound scanning

10. Ultrasound echolocation can be used by engineers to locate defects in long pipes. The ultrasound signal is sent down a pipe. The receiver receives two signals, one after 90 ms (the defect) and the other after 135 ms (the end of the pipe).

Calculate the distance between the **end** of the pipe and the defect

Speed of waves in pipe = 5 000 m/s

GCSE
ELECTROMAGNETIC WAVES

The electromagnetic spectrum consists of all the possible wavelengths and frequencies of electromagnetic radiation, including visible light.

1. Put the following types of electromagnetic radiation in order from the smallest wavelength to longest wavelength.

    Microwave   Gamma   Ultraviolet   X-ray   Visible Light   Radio   Infrared

2. State the velocity of all electromagnetic (EM) waves in a vacuum.

3. Identify the type of EM radiation that transfers the most energy.

4. EM waves are the only waves that can travel through a vacuum.

    a. True   b. False

5. State the type(s) of EM wave(s) that can be used in communication.

6. Write down what FM, LW and MW stand for in terms of radio communications.

7. Compare microwaves to radio waves when used for communications.

8. State the type of EM radiation that every object emits.

9. Name the seven colours that make up visible (white) light from shortest to longest wavelength.

10. Visible light has a wavelength range of approximately 400 nm – 700 nm. Calculate the approximate range of frequencies for visible light (1 nm = 1 x 10⁻⁹ m).

11. EM radiation with a wavelength less than that of visible light can be damaging to skin cells because it is ionising. Name the three types of EM radiation this corresponds to.

12. Explain why ionising radiation can be harmful to animals and humans.

13. Write down some uses we have for X-rays.

14. Explain why radiographers stand behind a protective screen when they take an X-ray.

15. Explain how X-rays can be produced.

16. Match the EM radiation to the object they are absorbed by.

   Microwave   Gamma   Ultraviolet   X-ray   Visible light

   Skin   Water molecules in food   Several metres of lead   Black cloth   Bone

17. Describe how microwaves heat up food.

18. Calculate the wavelength of EM radiation that has a frequency of 2.3 x 10^{15} Hz.

19. Calculate the frequency of EM radiation that has a wavelength of 9.8 x 10^{-9} m.

GCSE
REFRACTION

As a wave passes over the boundary between one medium and another it changes speed. If the wave is not travelling exactly perpendicular to the boundary then it will also change direction.

1. Describe how the angle of refraction differs from the angle of incidence if the wave speeds up as it crosses a boundary.

2. Write down i) the colour of light that refracts the most and ii) the colour of light that refracts the least.

   i)   ii)

3. A wave can be thought of as being made up of parallel wavefronts, one wavelength apart. Use this description of waves to explain in detail why refraction occurs.

4. The diagram on the right shows a light ray incident on a perspex block.

   a. Write down whether the light will speed up or slow down as it crosses the boundary from air to perspex

   b. Write down whether the light will speed up or slow down as it crosses the boundary from perspex to air

   c. Hence, complete the diagram as light travels from air, through a perspex block and out into air again

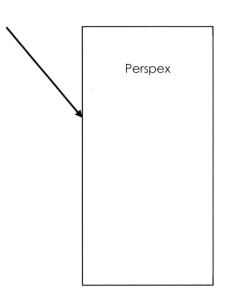

Perspex

5. Complete the diagram showing where a light ray refracts at the surface of two glass blocks.

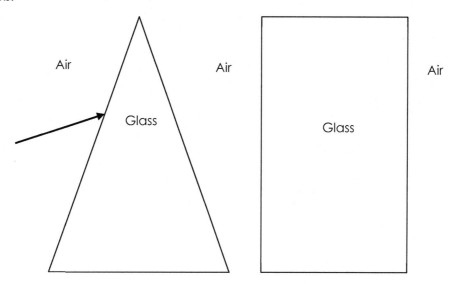

6. Double glazed windows can sometimes fill up with water if there is a leak. Complete the diagram showing where a light ray refracts at the surfaces of air, glass and water. Light travels fastest in air, then water and slowest in glass.

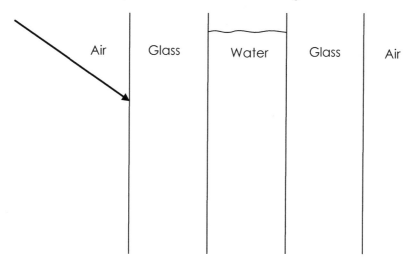

7. Explain, in terms of refraction, and by completing the diagram, why shining a beam of white light at a triangular prism produces a beam of light that is all the colours of the rainbow. Use your answer to question 2.

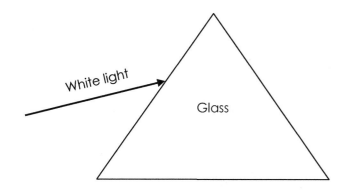

physics online

GCSE
CONVEX (CONVERGING) LENSES

A convex (or converging) lens uses refraction to bend light in order to either focus (cameras) or disperse (magnifying glass) light.

1. Describe the shape of a convex lens.

2. Write down the name of the point in space that a convex lens focuses light to.

3. Write down the name of the distance between the centre of a convex lens and the point named in question 2 above.

4. Describe what happens to light that passes through the centre of a convex lens.

5. Complete and the following diagrams below for light from an object being focused by a convex lens.

   a.

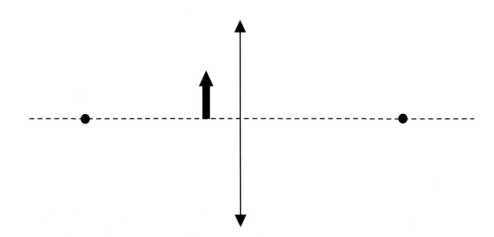

b.

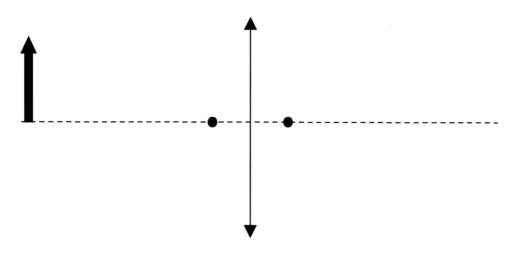

c.

6. Describe the image produced of an object with a convex lens (include the image's size, orientation, position and whether or not it is real or virtual) when:

   a. The object is less than one focal length from the lens

   b. The object is a long way from the lens

GCSE
CONCAVE (DIVERGING) LENSES

A concave (or diverging) lens uses refraction to bend light in order to diverge (or spread out) light incident on it.

1. Describe the shape of a concave lens.

2. A concave lens diverges light so it spreads out. Explain the meaning of the focal point of a concave lens.

3. Explain what is meant by a virtual image.

4. Explain how we can see a virtual image if it is in fact, virtual.

5. Complete and label the following diagrams below for light from an object being diverged by a concave lens:

    a.

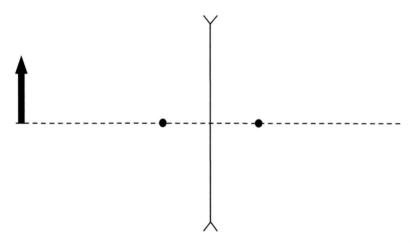

b.

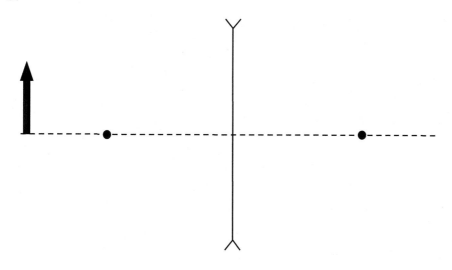

c.

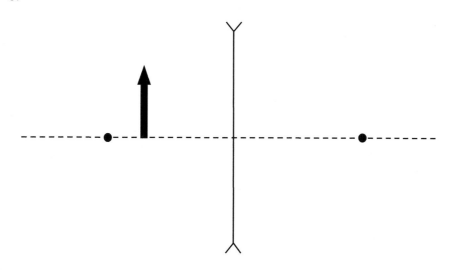

6. Describe the image produced by a concave lens when the object is at a distance greater than the focal length. Include the image's size, orientation, position and whether or not it is real or virtual.

7. Compare how your answer for question 8 would be different if a convex (converging) lens was used instead of a concave (diverging) lens. See your convex lens worksheet for guidance.

GCSE
COLOUR

The range of colours we see around us are our brain's perception of light (electromagnetic radiation) with different colours corresponding to different wavelengths and frequencies.

1. In Physics, the three primary colours of light are slightly different from those taught when painting in Art. Write these 3 colours down.

2. Write down the three secondary colours of light and what combination of primary colours makes them.

3. Write down what colour is made when all three primary colours are combined in equal proportion.

4. Explain if the same occurs when all three secondary colours are combined in equal proportion.

5. Explain how a yellow light source and a blue light source can make white light when combined.

6. Explain why a tree appears green (ignoring GCSE Biology).

7. Describe what a colour filter does and how it works.

8. Write down what colour a tree would appear if looked at through a green filter.

9. Write down what colour a tree would appear if looked at through a red filter.

10. One of the first people to investigate colour theory was Italian Leonardo da Vinci. The Italian flag is shown below. Sketch the Italian flag if it was observed as follows:

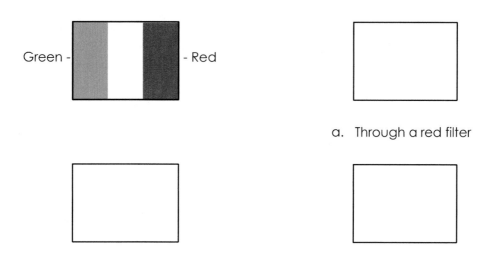

Green -   - Red

a. Through a red filter

b. Through a green filter

c. Through a blue filter

11. Complete the drawings below showing white light reflected from a surface. Complete the ray diagram and label the colour of light reflected.

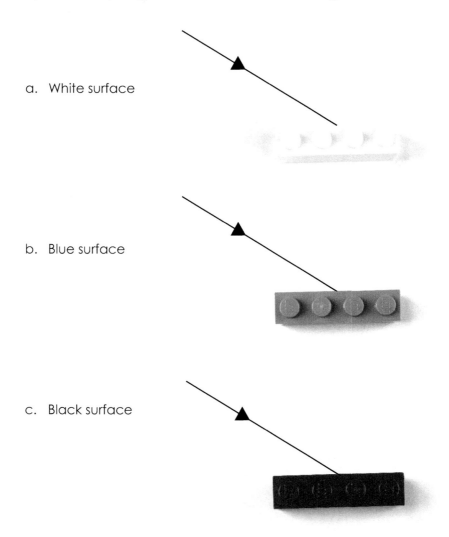

a. White surface

b. Blue surface

c. Black surface

Magnetism and Electromagnetism

GCSE
MAGNETIC FIELDS

Every magnet has a magnetic field around it. Within the magnetic field, other magnets and magnetic materials experience a force.

1. Write down the names given to the two ends of a magnet.

2. Write down which end of a magnet a compass points to.

3. Describe how Earth's magnetic field is vital for life to exist on Earth.

4. Traditional bar magnets are an example of a permanent magnet. Explain what is meant by a permanent magnet.

5. A magnetic field can be displayed using field lines. Write down the direction that field lines point in.

6. Sketch the shape of a magnetic field around a bar magnet.

7. Explain what it represents when magnetic field lines are close together.

8. Explain what it means when a magnet's field lines are parallel and equally spaced out.

9. A moving charged particle will produce a magnetic field. Hence explain why a current flowing through a wire produces a magnetic field.

10. Explain what a solenoid is.

11. Describe the shape of a solenoid's magnetic field, including inside and outside the solenoid and where the field is strongest.

12. Explain why an iron core is often placed in a solenoid.

13. Draw the magnetic field lines around the following magnetic objects:

    a. Current carrying wire (conventional current going into the page)

    b. The Earth

GCSE
THE MOTOR EFFECT

A wire that carries current through an external magnetic field experiences a force at right angles to both the current flow and the magnetic field. We use Fleming's left hand rule to determine in which direction this force acts.

1. Below is a picture of the hand position for Fleming's left hand rule. Label each of the fingers/arrows with what they represent.

2. Describe the direction of the three variables relative to each other i.e. the angle between them.

3. In a permanent magnetic field explain how the force on a current carrying wire changes if the current changes direction.

Below is the equation for the force acting on a current carrying wire in a magnetic field.

F = BIL

4. Write down the equation using words rather than symbols and name the units that each of the four variables in the equation are measured in.

5. Calculate the force acting on the following:

   a. A 10 cm wire with a current of 2.0 A in a magnetic field of 0.45 T

   b. A 2.0 m wire with a current of 10 A in a magnetic field of 8.0 T

   c. A 2.0 m wire with a current of 10 kA in a magnetic field of 8.0 mT

6. Below are three diagrams of current carrying wires within a magnetic field. Use Fleming's left hand rule to determine the direction of motion of each wire.

a.

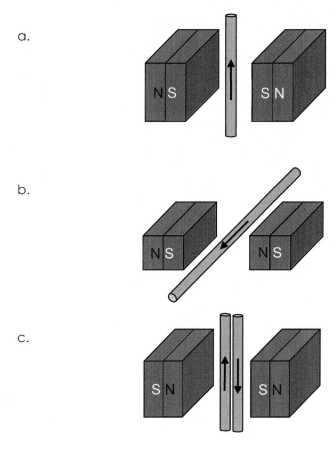

b.

c.

7. Describe the parts of a simple electric motor.

8. Explain the role of a split ring commutator in a DC motor and how it enables the motor to spin continuously in the same direction.

9. Explain how a loudspeaker uses the motor effect to produce sound waves.

GCSE
THE GENERATOR EFFECT

The generator effect can be thought of as the opposite of the motor effect; by moving a conductor in a magnetic field we can induce a potential difference and hence a current.

1. Compare the similarities and differences between the motor and generator effects.

2. Describe a way of generating a current using a wire and permanent magnet.

3. Write down three things that would induce a greater potential difference and therefore a greater current.

4. Describe what happens when a plastic object falls through a copper tube.

5. Explain why a magnet falling through a copper tube falls very slowly.

6. Alternators and dynamos are two types of generators. Describe the main difference between them.

7. Describe the shape of an alternating current (AC) graph with respect to time.

8. Describe how we can increase the amplitude of the AC output.

9. Describe how we can decrease the frequency of the AC output.

10. Speakers and microphones are often thought of as very different. Describe how speakers and microphones are actually quite similar.

11. Mains electricity runs at 230V and is an alternating current source. Write down the frequency of mains AC.

12. Sketch the graph of potential difference against time for a generator if under the following conditions:

    a. The magnetic field strength is doubled

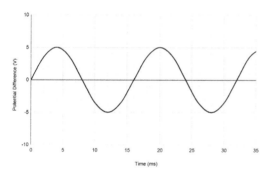

    b. The coil is rotated half as quickly

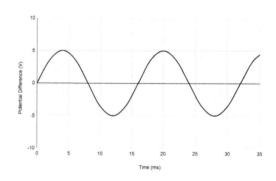

    c. The magnet direction is reversed

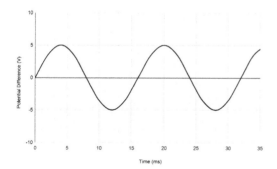

    d. The coil is rotated twice as quickly **and** the magnetic field strength is halved

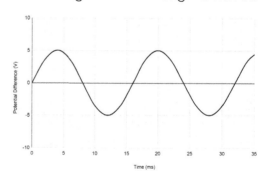

Transformers are used to reduce the power loss in the national grid. Below is an equation for power loss in a current carrying wire.

$$P = I^2R$$

1. Write down the equation using words rather than symbols and name the units that each of the three variables in the equation are measured in.

2. Calculate the power loss of:

   a. 10 A flowing through a 270 Ω resistor

   b. 1.0 A flowing through a 270 Ω resistor

3. Explain the effect of reducing the current through a wire.

4. A simple transformer includes an iron core and two separate coils of wire. Describe how this apparatus is put together to produce a transformer.

5. Explain the importance of the core being iron.

6. Describe the magnetic field produced by a coil of wire carrying an alternating current.

7. Describe in order, the steps that cause an alternating current in one coil to produce an alternating current in a second coil. (Think about the magnetic field, potential difference and current of both coils).

An equation used with transformers is:

$$V_p/V_s = n_p/n_s$$

8. Write down the equation using words rather than symbols and name the units that each of the four variables in the equation are measured in.

9. In a step-down transformer the number of turns in the primary coil is 980 compared to the secondary coil which only has 175. The output is 1.0 kV, calculate the input voltage.

10. The number of turns in a primary coil of a transformer is 135. The transformer steps the voltage up from an input of 12.5V to 230V. Calculate the number of turns in the secondary coil.

GCSE
TRANSFORMERS 2

The ratio of potential differences across two coils of wire in a transformer is dependent on the ratio of the number of turns of both coils. This affects the ratio of currents in each coil.

1. Write down the meaning of the law of conservation of energy.

2. Explain how the law of conservation of energy applies to conservation of power.

3. Write down the equation for electrical power in terms of current and potential difference (voltage).

4. In a transformer, there are two separate circuits, each with its own potential difference and current. Write down how the power of the two circuits are related in an ideal transformer (the power in the primary coil, P_p, and the power in the secondary coil, P_s)

5. Hence derive an equation relating the potential difference and current of both primary and secondary coils.

6. Explain how increasing or decreasing the potential difference across one circuit affects that circuit's current.

7. Household electrical items use transformers in their chargers. A phone charger transforms mains electricity to 5.2 V and 8.6 A. Calculate the current drawn in the mains (230 V) when the phone is plugged in.

8. A transformer has a primary current of 210 A, a secondary current of 7.6 A and a secondary voltage of 1.9 kV. Calculate the primary voltage.

9. The ratio between the number of turns in the primary coil of a transformer to the secondary coil is 85. Calculate the secondary voltage if the primary voltage is 1700 mV.

10. Explain why transfers are used in the National Grid.

11. The primary coil in a transformer has 710 turns whilst the secondary coil has 63. Calculate the current induced in the secondary coil if the primary current is 800 mA.

Space

GCSE
LIFECYCLE OF STARS

All stars are born in the same way but there are many different ways in which they end their lives, depending on their mass.

1. State the most abundant element in the Universe.

2. Describe what a nebula is.

3. Hot, dense regions form in nebulas. State what these regions are called.

4. State the process that binds hydrogen nuclei together.

5. Explain how the answer to question 4 prevents a star from collapsing.

6. Describe how hydrogen nuclei (protons) undergoing fusion can produce helium nuclei (2 protons and 2 neutrons)

7. Describe what happens to an average star when the hydrogen fuel starts to run out and what it uses as fuel instead.

8. Describe what happens to an average sized star once all the fuel has run out.

9. Explain why a more massive star has a shorter life than a smaller star.

physics online

gcsephysicsonline.com/**stars**

10. Write down the heaviest element that a massive star can form during its main sequence.

11. Explain why some elements cannot be produced by fusion in main sequence stars.

12. Explain how the elements that cannot be produced in main sequence stars are produced.

13. State what is left behind after a supernova if the mass of the remaining material is so great that it cannot support itself.

14. Write down what is at the centre of our galaxy, the Milky Way.

15. State the volume, in metres cubed, of a black hole.

GCSE
THE BIG BANG

It all started with a Big Bang!

1. Describe how we can split white light into a spectrum of colours.

2. Describe what an absorption spectrum is.

3. Explain what the black lines in a star's absorption spectrum tell us about the star.

4. Explain why a galaxy's absorption spectrum might be shifted, and to what end of the spectrum it is shifted towards.

5. Describe the relationship between a galaxy's distance from us and how much its light is redshifted by.

6. If every galaxy's absorption spectrum is redshifted, explain what this tells us about the Universe.

7. If the Universe is expanding, explain why this is one piece of evidence for the Big Bang.

8. State what CMBR stands for.

9. Explain what the expansion of the Universe has done to this radiation.

10. Explain why CMBR is a further piece of evidence for the Big Bang.

11. Explain what will happen to the wavelength of the CMBR in the future as the Universe keeps expanding.

12. Describe the evidence for dark matter.

13. Write down what is actually happening to the rate of expansion of the Universe.

14. Describe the evidence for dark energy.

GCSE
ENERGY STORES AND TRANSFERS

Energy can be stored and transferred in different ways.

1. Write down the unit for measuring energy.

J (the joule)

2. Write down eight different energy stores.

- Chemical
- Thermal — sometimes called 'internal'
- Kinetic
- Magnetic
- Gravitational Potential
- Nuclear
- Electric Potential
- Electrostatic

3. Write down the four main types of energy transfer between stores. (Hint: HERM)

- Heating
- Electrical
- Radiation — Light (and all EM waves) and sound
- Mechanical

4. A teddy bear is thrown vertically upwards from the ground. It has an initial kinetic energy of 68 J.

a. As the bear travels upwards, describe what happens to the value of energy in the kinetic store

It decreases as its velocity decreases

b. The kinetic energy is transferred to a different store of energy, write down the name of this store

Gravitational potential energy store

c. Write down the name of the type of energy transfer responsible for transferring the kinetic energy to this new energy store

Mechanical

d. Write down the value of energy in this new store when the bear is at the top of its flight path (at the highest point)

68 J assuming no energy losses

---

5. For the following examples, name the store(s) that the energy is stored in:

a. A bow that has been pulled back

Elastic potential store

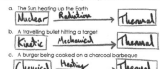

b. The nucleus of an oxygen atom

Nuclear store

c. The south poles of two bar magnets being held close together

Magnetic store

d. A hot hotdog

Chemical and thermal stores

6. For the following examples, name the initial and final energy stores as well as the method responsible for transferring energy from the initial to the final store:

a. The Sun heating up the Earth

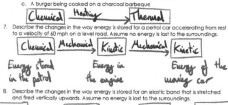

Nuclear →Radiation→ Thermal

b. A travelling bullet hitting a target

Kinetic →Mechanical→ Thermal

c. A burger being cooked on a charcoal barbeque

Chemical →Heating→ Thermal

7. Describe the changes in the way energy is stored for a petrol car accelerating from rest to a velocity of 60 mph on a level road. Assume no energy is lost to the surroundings.

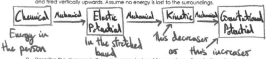

Chemical →Mechanical→ Kinetic →Mechanical→ Kinetic

Energy stored in the petrol | Energy in the engine | Energy of the moving car

8. Describe the changes in the way energy is stored for an elastic band that is stretched and fired vertically upwards. Assume no energy is lost to the surroundings.

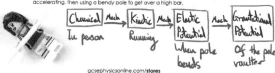

Chemical →Mechanical→ Elastic Potential →Mechanical→ Kinetic →Mechanical→ Gravitational Potential

Energy in the person | In the stretched band | This decreases as this increases

9. Describe the changes in the way energy is stored for a pole vaulter, starting at rest, accelerating, then using a bendy pole to get over a high bar.

Chemical →Mech→ Kinetic →Mech→ Elastic Potential →Mech→ Gravitational Potential

In person | Running | When pole bends | Of the pole vaulter

GCSE
ENERGY CONSERVATION AND EFFICIENCY

Energy cannot be created or destroyed.

efficiency = useful output energy transfer / total input energy transfer

1. Write down the name given to energy that is not usefully transferred.

Wasted energy

2. Write down two different ways efficiency can be displayed in.

Percentage or a decimal (75% or 0.75)

3. Describe what happens to energy that is not usefully transferred, including the store it is most commonly transferred to.

It is dissipated to the surroundings — thermal store

4. Write down another version of the equation for efficiency concerning power.

efficiency = useful output power / total input power

5. Calculate the percentage efficiency of a machine that has:

a. A total energy input of 40 J and a useful energy output of 22 J

efficiency = 22/40 = 0.55 or 55%

b. A total energy input of 124 J and a useful energy output of 43.4 J

efficiency = 43.4/124 = 0.35 or 35%

c. A total power input of 2.4 W and a useful power output of 0.96 W

efficiency = 0.96/2.4 = 0.40 or 40%

6. Explain why electric heaters can have very high efficiencies.

Their 'wasted' energy is dissipated to the thermal store of the room.

7. Explain what is meant by thermal conductivity, giving examples of good and bad thermal conductors.

Thermal conductivity is a measure of the rate of heat transfer through a material.

Good conductors — metals

Bad conductors — glass and plastic (good insulators)

---

8. An ultra-ultra-bouncy ball is dropped from a height of 12.0 m. After it bounces once, the ball reaches a height of 10.8 m.

a. Calculate the efficiency of the ball as a percentage

efficiency = 10.8/12.0 = 0.900 or 90.0% (3sf)

b. Calculate the height reached after the ball bounces i) twice, ii) three times and iii) six times

i. 1st 2nd
12.0 × 0.9 × 0.9 = 9.72 m

ii. 3rd
12.0 × 0.9 × 0.9 × 0.9 = 8.748 ≃ 8.75 m

iii. 12.0 × 0.9⁶ = 6.38 m

9. A rocket's engine uses 170 kJ worth of fuel in the first stage of taking off. The rocket itself gains 36.0 kJ of kinetic energy as well as 32.0 kJ of gravitational potential energy.

a. Calculate the efficiency of the rocket's engine

efficiency = (36.0 + 32.0)/170 = 0.400 or 40.0%
— you can leave them both in kJ

Before the next take-off, the rocket's engine has its efficiency increased by 10%.

b. Calculate the new useful output energy transfer

efficiency = 0.400 × 1.10 = 0.440

useful E output = efficiency × E input = 0.440 × 170 = 74.8 kJ

10. An electric car is used to deliver pizzas. The car's efficiency is 0.73 and its useful power output is 8.7 kW.

a. Calculate the power input

power input = power output / efficiency = 8.7/0.73 ≃ 11.92 ≃ 12 kW

The power input is increased by 25% but this decreases the efficiency to 0.63.

b. Calculate the new useful power output. Comment if the useful power output is now greater than when it was before

power output = efficiency × power input
= 0.63 × (11.92 × 1.25) A higher output!
= 9.385 ≃ 9.4 kW (2sf)

The energy stored by moving objects.

kinetic energy = ½ x mass x velocity²

1. Write the equation in symbols and name the units that each of the three variables in the equation are measured in.

$$E_K = \frac{1}{2}mv^2$$

J   kg   m/s

2. Calculate the kinetic energy of:

a. A 3.0 kg mass moving at 4.0 m/s

$$E_K = \frac{1}{2}mv^2 = \frac{1}{2} \times 3.0 \times 4.0^2 = \underline{24 \text{ J}}$$

b. A 6.0 kg mass moving at 4.0 m/s

$$E_K = \frac{1}{2}mv^2 = \frac{1}{2} \times 6.0 \times 4.0^2 = \underline{48 \text{ J}}$$

c. A 3.0 kg mass moving at 8.0 m/s

$$E_K = \frac{1}{2}mv^2 = \frac{1}{2} \times 3.0 \times 8.0^2 = \underline{96 \text{ J}}$$

d. Compare what happens to the kinetic energy of an object when its mass is doubled versus what happens when its velocity is doubled

$$2 \times m \rightarrow 2 \times E_K \qquad 2 \times V \rightarrow 4 \times E_K$$

3. Rearrange the equation to i) make **m** the subject, then ii) rearrange to make **v** the subject.

i) $$m = \frac{2E_K}{v^2}$$ ii) $$v = \sqrt{\frac{2E_K}{m}}$$

4. Fill in the table with the missing values (to 3 sf).

Kinetic Energy (J)	Mass (kg)	Velocity (m/s)	Calculations
62.5	5.00	5.00	$E_K = \frac{1}{2}mv^2 = \frac{1}{2} \times 5.00 \times 5.00^2 = 62.5$
25.0	5.00	10.0	$E_K = \frac{1}{2}mv^2 = \frac{1}{2} \times 5.00 \times 10.0^2 = 25$
243	6.00	9.00	$v = \sqrt{2E_K/m} = \sqrt{6 \times 243}/6.00 = 9$
243	4.02	11.0	$m = 2E_K/v^2 = 2 \times 243/11.0^2 = 4.017$
243	0.600	28.5	$v = \sqrt{2E_K/m} = \sqrt{2 \times 243/0.600} = 28.46$
42.0	3.92	4.63	$m = 2E_K/v^2 = 2 \times 42.0/4.63^2 = 3.918$

5. A tennis ball has a mass of 58 g and is served at 42 m/s.

a. Calculate the kinetic energy stored by the ball as it leaves the tennis racket

$$E_K = \frac{1}{2}mv^2 = \frac{1}{2} \times 0.058 \times 42^2 = 51.156 \simeq \underline{51 \text{ J}} \; (2sf)$$

The ball is hit harder such that it stores twice as much kinetic energy.

b. Calculate how fast the ball would need to be travelling

$$E_K = 2 \times 51.156 = 102.312 \text{ J}$$

$$v = \sqrt{\frac{2E_K}{m}} = \sqrt{\frac{2 \times 102.312}{0.058}} = 59.397 \simeq \underline{59 \text{ m/s}}$$

A baseball has a mass of 160 g and stores the same kinetic energy as a tennis ball that is travelling at 50 m/s.

c. Calculate how fast the baseball would need to be travelling

Tennis ball → $$E_K = \frac{1}{2}mv^2 = \frac{1}{2} \times 0.058 \times 50^2 = 72.5 \text{ J}$$

Baseball → $$v = \sqrt{\frac{2E_K}{m}} = \sqrt{\frac{2 \times 72.5}{0.160}} = 30.10 \simeq \underline{30 \text{ m/s}}$$

6. The International Space Station (ISS) orbits at 7.66 km/s and has a mass of 420 tonnes.

a. Calculate the ISS's kinetic energy   (1 tonne = 1000 kg)

$$E_K = \frac{1}{2}mv^2 = \frac{1}{2} \times 420 \times 10^3 \times 7660^2 = 1.23219 \times 10^{13}$$
$$\simeq \underline{1.23 \times 10^{13} \text{ J}}$$

A 4.30 tonne geostationary communications satellite orbits at 3.07 km/s.

b. Calculate the satellite's kinetic energy

$$E_K = \frac{1}{2}mv^2 = \frac{1}{2} \times 4.30 \times 10^3 \times 3070^2 = 2.02635 \times 10^{10}$$
$$\simeq \underline{2.03 \times 10^{10} \text{ J}}$$

c. Compare how much energy is stored by the ISS to the communication satellite. give your answer as a ratio

$$ratio = \frac{E_K \text{ of ISS}}{E_K \text{ of sat}} = \frac{1.23219 \times 10^{13}}{2.02635 \times 10^{10}} = \underline{608:1}$$

An asteroid travels at the same speed as the ISS in part a. (7.66 km/s), but possesses the same kinetic energy as the satellite in part b.

d. Calculate the asteroid's mass

$$m = \frac{2E_K}{v^2} = \frac{2 \times 2.02635 \times 10^{10}}{7660^2} = 690.7$$
$$\simeq \underline{691 \text{ kg}}$$

The energy stored by objects in a gravitational field.

gravitational potential energy = mass x gravitational field strength x height

1. Name the units that each of the four variables in the equation are measured in.

J   kg   N/kg   m

2. Write down the value of Earth's gravitational field strength (to one decimal place).

9.8 N/kg   sometimes 10 N/kg is used for GCSE

3. Calculate, using your answer to question 2, the gravitational potential energy of:

a. A 4.0 kg mass, 7.9 m above the Earth's surface   (2sf)

$$E_p = mgh = 4.0 \times 9.8 \times 7.9 = 309.68 \simeq \underline{310 \text{ J}}$$

b. A 3.0 kg mass, 16 m above the Earth's surface

$$E_p = mgh = 3.0 \times 9.8 \times 16 = 470.4 \simeq \underline{470 \text{ J}}$$

4. i) Rearrange the equation to make **m** the subject, ii) rearrange to make **h** the subject and iii) rearrange to make **g** the subject.

i) $$m = \frac{E_p}{gh}$$ ii) $$h = \frac{E_p}{mg}$$ iii) $$g = \frac{E_p}{mh}$$

5. Fill in the table with the missing values (to 2 sf).

E_p (J)	m (kg)	g (N/kg)	h (m)	Calculations
150	5.0	9.8	3.0	$E_p = mgh = 5.0 \times 9.8 \times 3.0 = 147$
2100	7.5	9.8	28	$E_p = mgh = 7.5 \times 9.8 \times 28 = 2058$
350	10	1.6	22	$h = E_p/mg = 350/10 \times 1.6 = 21.88$
200	6.0	9.8	3.4	$h = E_p/mg = 200/6.0 \times 9.8 = 3.401$
810	4.4	9.8	19	$m = E_p/gh = 810/9.8 \times 19 = 4.350$
240	250	1.6	0.6	$m = E_p/gh = 240/1.6 \times 0.6 = 250$
34	0.2	27	6.3	$g = E_p/mh = 34/0.2 \times 6.3 = 26.98$
89	18	3.3	1.5	$g = E_p/mh = 89/18 \times 1.5 = 3.296$

6. A cannonball has a mass of 13 kg and is fired vertically upwards from the surface of the Earth to a height of 27 m. (use g = 9.8 N/kg at the surface of Earth.)

a. Calculate the cannonball's maximum gravitational potential energy

$$E_p = mgh = 13 \times 9.8 \times 27 = 3439.8$$
$$\simeq \underline{3400 \text{ J}} \; (2sf)$$

The cannonball is fired upwards such that it stores double the maximum gravitational potential energy.

b. Calculate how high the ball is fired

$$E_p \propto h \qquad 2 \times E_p \text{ means } 2 \times h$$
$$2 \times 27 = \underline{54 \text{ m}}$$

7. An alien flies at a height of 123 m above its home planet's surface. The alien has a mass of 12 kg and stores 790 J of gravitational potential energy. Calculate the value of 'g' for this planet.

$$g = \frac{E_p}{mh} = \frac{710}{12 \times 123} = 0.5352 \simeq \underline{0.54 \text{ N/kg}}$$

8. An astronaut on the surface of the Moon has a mass of 75 kg. They pick up a rock which has a mass of 1.5 kg. (The value of g on the Moon = 1.6 N/kg.)

a. Calculate the increase in gravitational potential energy of the astronaut holding the rock if they jump a height of 1.2 m

$$E_p = mgh = (75 + 1.5) \times 1.6 \times 1.2$$
$$= 146.88 \simeq \underline{150 \text{ J}} \; (2sf)$$

The astronaut throws the rock vertically upwards such that it stores the same maximum gravitational potential energy as the astronaut and rock combined in part (a.)

b. Calculate the rock's increase in height

$$h = \frac{E_p}{mg} = \frac{146.88}{1.5 \times 1.6} = 61.2 \simeq \underline{61 \text{ m}}$$

The astronaut picks up another rock and throws it vertically upwards. This rock reaches the same height as in (b.) but stores 35 J more gravitational potential energy than in (a.)

c. Calculate this rock's mass

$$m = \frac{E_p}{gh} = \frac{146.88 + 35}{1.6 \times 61.2} = 1.857 \simeq \underline{1.9 \text{ kg}}$$

GCSE
ELASTIC POTENTIAL ENERGY

The energy stored by objects which have been elastically deformed (stretched or compressed within the limit of proportionality).

$$E_e = \frac{1}{2}ke^2$$

1. Write down the equation using words rather than symbols and name the units:

J elastic potential energy $= \frac{1}{2} \times$ spring constant (N/m) $\times$ extension^2 (m)

2. Calculate the elastic potential energy stored by:

a. A spring with a spring constant of 72.0 N/m that is extended by 0.300 m

$$E_e = \frac{1}{2}ke^2 = \frac{1}{2} \times 72.0 \times 0.300^2 = \underline{3.24 \text{ J}} \quad (3sf)$$

b. A spring with a spring constant of 72.0 N/m that is extended by 0.150 m

$$E_e = \frac{1}{2}ke^2 = \frac{1}{2} \times 72.0 \times 0.150^2 = \underline{0.810 \text{ J}}$$

c. A spring with a spring constant of 36.0 N/m that is extended by 0.300 m

$$E_e = \frac{1}{2}ke^2 = \frac{1}{2} \times 36.0 \times 0.300^2 = \underline{1.62 \text{ J}}$$

d. Compare what happens to the elastic potential energy of a spring when its extension is doubled versus when its spring constant is doubled

$$2 \times e \rightarrow 4 \times E_e \qquad 2 \times k \rightarrow 2 \times E_e$$

3. i) Rearrange the equation to make k the subject, then ii) rearrange to make e the subject.

i) $$k = \frac{2E_e}{e^2}$$

ii) $$e = \sqrt{\frac{2E_e}{k}}$$

4. Fill in the table with the missing values (to 2 sf).

E_e (J)	k (N/m)	Extension (m)	Calculations
3.6	5.0	1.2	$E_e = \frac{1}{2}ke^2 = \frac{1}{2} \times 5.0 \times 1.2^2 = 3.6$
6.9	17	0.90	$E_e = \frac{1}{2}ke^2 = \frac{1}{2} \times 17 \times 0.90^2 = 6.8885$
110	1400	0.40	$k = 2E_e/e^2 = 2 \times 110/0.40^2 = 1375$
280	1600	0.60	$k = 2E_e/e^2 = 2 \times 280/0.60^2 = 1556$
240	78	2.5	$e = \sqrt{2E_e/k} = \sqrt{2 \times 240/78} = 2.481$

gcsephysicsonline.com/**elastic**

---

5. A bird feeder is suspended on the end of a spring. The spring has a spring constant of 129 N/m and has an original length of 12.0 cm. When the bird feeder, which is full of bird food, is hung from the spring, the spring extends to 17.0 cm.

a. Calculate the extension of the spring

$$0.170 - 0.120 = 0.0500 \text{ m}$$

b. Calculate the elastic potential energy stored in the spring

$$E_e = \frac{1}{2}ke^2 = \frac{1}{2} \times 129 \times 0.0500^2 = 0.16125 \approx \underline{0.161 \text{ J}} \quad (3sf)$$

Over the course of a few days, all the bird food is eaten. The elastic potential energy of the spring is now a quarter of what it was in part (b.)

c. Calculate the new extension of the spring, and hence its final length

$$E_e = \frac{0.16125}{4} = 0.0403125 \qquad e = \sqrt{\frac{2E_e}{k}} = \sqrt{\frac{2 \times 0.0403125}{129}}$$

$$e = 0.0250 \text{ m} \rightarrow l = 0.145 \text{ m}$$

6. A 10 cm long spring, with a spring constant of 27 N/m, is used to reload the ball in a pinball machine. The spring is compressed by 4.0 cm by a mechanism in the machine and then let go.

a. Calculate the elastic potential energy stored in the spring

$$E_e = \frac{1}{2}ke^2 = \frac{1}{2} \times 27 \times 0.040^2 = 0.0216 \approx \underline{0.022 \text{ J}} \quad (2sf)$$

A new spring is fitted into the machine. It only needs to be compressed by 3.0 cm to store the same amount of elastic potential energy as the previous spring.

b. Calculate the spring constant of this new spring

$$k = \frac{2E_e}{e^2} = \frac{2 \times 0.0216}{0.030^2} = \underline{48 \text{ N/m}}$$

The owner of the game wants to double the potential energy stored in this new spring.

c. Calculate the compression of the spring needed in order to achieve this

$$e = \sqrt{\frac{2E_e}{k}} = \sqrt{\frac{2 \times (2 \times 0.0216)}{48}} = 0.04243 \approx \underline{0.042 \text{ m}}$$

A child, eating a 30 cm long gummy snake which has a spring constant of 15 N/m, comes to play on the machine. The child pulls the gummy snake until its length has doubled.

d. Calculate the elastic potential energy stored in the gummy snake assuming the gummy snake has been stretched within the limit of proportionality

$$E_e = \frac{1}{2}ke^2 = \frac{1}{2} \times 15 \times 0.30^2$$

$$= 0.675 \approx \underline{0.68 \text{ J}}$$

GCSE
POWER

Power is the rate of transfer of energy.

power = energy transferred / time

1. Write down the equation using symbols rather than words.

$$P = \frac{E}{t}$$

2. Name the units that each of the three variables in the equation are measured in.

W   J   s

3. Calculate the power for:

a. 780 J transferred over 12 s

$$P = \frac{E}{t} = 780/12 = \underline{65 \text{ W}}$$

b. 0.30 J transferred over 0.050 s

$$P = \frac{E}{t} = 0.30/0.050 = \underline{6.0 \text{ W}}$$

c. 12 kJ transferred over one minute

$$P = \frac{E}{t} = 12000/60 = \underline{200 \text{ W}} \quad \text{ALWAYS convert time to seconds}$$

d. 5.4 MJ transferred over one hour

$$P = \frac{E}{t} = 5400000/60 \times 60 = \underline{1500 \text{ W}}$$

4. Rearrange the original equation to make E the subject, then ii) rearrange to make t the subject.

i) $$E = Pt$$

ii) $$t = \frac{E}{P}$$

5. Fill in the table with the missing values (to an appropriate number of sf).

Power (W)	Energy Transferred (J)	Time (s)	Calculations
6.58 (3sf)	78.9	12.0	$P = E/t = 78.9/12.0 = 6.575$
760	380	0.50	$t = E/P = 380/760 = 0.5$
8.8 (2sf)	2200	250	$t = E/P = 2200/8.8 = 250$
1800	900	0.50	$E = Pt = 1800 \times 0.50 = 900$
89	5900	66	$E = Pt = 89 \times 66 = 5874$

gcsephysicsonline.com/**power**

---

6. A battery transfers 1.5 J of energy over 28 s.

a. Calculate the power of the battery at this time

$$P = \frac{E}{t} = 1.5/28 = 0.05357 = \underline{0.054 \text{ W}} \quad (2sf)$$

A different batter transfers 2.3 J of energy over 34 s.

b. Calculate if this battery has a greater power than the first battery

$$P = \frac{E}{t} = 2.3/34 = 0.06765 = \underline{0.068 \text{ W}} \quad \therefore \text{greater power}$$

7. An office photocopier requires a power input of 0.80 W when it is left on standby. The photocopier is left on standby overnight for 9.0 hours.

a. Calculate how much energy is transferred by the photocopier

$$E = Pt = 0.80 \times (9.0 \times 60 \times 60)$$

$$= 25920$$

$$\approx \underline{26 \text{ kJ}} \quad (2sf)$$

No one uses the office over the weekend and sometimes the lights get left on. There are four 60 W bulbs in the office that are left on from 6.00 pm on Friday to 9.00 am on Monday.

b. Calculate the total energy transferred in this time by the four bulbs

$$E = Pt = 4 \times 60 \times (63 \times 60 \times 60) = 54\,432\,000$$

(no. of hours)

$$= \underline{54 \text{ MJ}}$$

8. An oven has a power rating of 2.4 kW. It takes half an hour to cook a fillet of fish.

a. Assuming all the energy is transferred to the fish, calculate its increase in thermal energy

$$E = Pt = 2400 \times (30 \times 60) = 4\,320\,000$$

$$= \underline{4.3 \text{ MJ}}$$

b. Calculate the power of a different oven, one that transfers the same amount of energy but in 4 minutes less

$$P = \frac{E}{t} = \frac{4\,320\,000}{(30-4) \times 60} = 2769 \approx \underline{2.8 \text{ kW}}$$

9. A crane uses a motor to lift heavy objects. The crane takes exactly 20 seconds to lift an object with a mass of 520 kg a height of 18 m.

Calculate the power of the crane's motor, assuming that all the energy is transferred usefully into lifting the object

$$E_p = mgh = 520 \times 9.8 \times 18 = 91\,728 \text{ J}$$

$$P = \frac{E}{t} = \frac{91\,728}{20} = 4586.4 \approx \underline{4.6 \text{ kW}}$$

gcsephysicsonline.com/**power**

GCSE
HEAT TRANSFER

A common process for heat transfer is conduction.

1. Write down how closely-packed particles are in a) a solid, b) a liquid and c) a gas.

   a. Closely packed together (and bonded together)
   b. Closely packed together
   c. Far apart

2. Describe what happens to the motion of the particles in: a) a solid. b) a liquid and c) a gas as the particles' temperature is increased.

   a. They vibrate with an increased amplitude

   b. They move about faster

   c. They move about even faster

3. Describe how heat is transferred via conduction.

   As particles heat up they vibrate more, they pass these vibrations onto their neighbours.

4. Using your answer to question 1, explain why solids are generally better thermal conductors than gases.

   The particles are closer together, so can pass the vibrations on quicker.

5. Most solids are made of neatly packed neutral atoms. Describe why metals are different.

   In a metal there are positive metal ions surrounded by negative free electrons.

6. Explain why your answer to question 5 means that metals are generally better thermal conductors than most solids.

   The electrons are free to move around so they can quickly move through the metal passing on the vibrations. This increases the rate of heat transfer.

gcsephysicsonline.com/**thermal-transfer**

7. Explain why copper is such a good thermal conductor.

   It has a large number of free electrons.

8. A student measures the temperature of a block of plastic and a block of metal. They both have a temperature of 20 °C but the student claims the metal block feels colder. Explain why.

   The metal is a better conductor, so it transfers the thermal energy away from the student quicker.

9. Write down the type of material that is a poor thermal conductor.

   An insulator

10. Write down the name given to a material's ability to thermally conduct heat.

    Thermal conductivity

11. Thermal conduction transfers thermal energy (heat). Explain why insulators can improve efficiency.

    They reduce the rate of energy transfer.

12. Double glazed windows have two panes of glass separated by a sealed layer of gas. Explain why double glazed windows are better insulators than single glazed windows.

    The gas, because the particles are far apart, is very good insulator.

13. Explain why the roof of a house has fibreglass insulation in it and why the ground floor does not have the same type of insulation underneath it.

    The fibreglass traps pockets of air which are a good insulator.
    It also reduces convection, where the hotter less dense air rises upwards.

gcsephysicsonline.com/**thermal-transfer**

GCSE
ENERGY RESOURCES

Energy can be stored in different ways and in different objects and materials. Energy can be transferred from these stores for use in transport, heating and our homes.

1. Name as many non-renewable energy sources as you can.

   Coal, oil, gas and nuclear fission.

2. Name as many renewable energy sources as you can.

   Solar, wind, geothermal, wave, tidal, biomass and hydroelectric.

3. Describe the main difference between non-renewable and renewable energy sources and how this makes renewable energy sources better for the planet.

   Once non-renewable resources have been used up they can't be replaced.

4. Briefly explain how a conventional power station converts the chemical energy in the fuels it burns until it is transferred electrically.

   The burning fuel heats up water which turns to steam. The steam causes a turbine to rotate which rotates a generator that induces a potential difference.

5. The National Grid has to cope with balancing supply with a rapidly changing demand. Describe why traditional power stations are useful for keeping up with demand.

   Gas power stations can rapidly start generating electricity to match the increased demand.

6. Write down the main drawbacks with traditional fossil fuel power stations.

   They release a lot of CO_2 into the atmosphere when they are burned.

gcsephysicsonline.com/**energy-resources**

7. Explain why some people think nuclear power stations are better for the environment than traditional power stations and why some think they are worse.

   Advantage No CO_2 released
   Disadvantage Disposing of waste + Risk of nuclear incident

8. Wind turbines also use a turbine to produce electricity. Explain how the design of a wind turbine means that no fuel is needed.

   The wind causes the blades to rotate, this is connected to a generator which then turns generating electricity.

9. Write down the problem with solar panels that wind turbines also share.

   They can not generate electricity if the weather conditions are not suitable (too cloudy or not windy)

10. Explain the benefit of hydroelectric power stations in terms of storing surplus energy.

    Surplus energy can be used to pump water to a greater height, increasing its gravitational potential energy store. Later this can be used to generate electricity.

11. Write down the problem with hydroelectric power stations that geothermal power stations also share.

    They can only be built in certain locations.

12. Wave power and tidal power are both renewable energy sources that also harness the power of water. Describe how i) waves and ii) tides can be harnessed.

    Waves - their movement causes small turbines to turn

    Tidal - water is held behind a tidal barrage, it is then released through turbines in a controlled way

13. Describe the problem harnessing tidal power poses to local wildlife.

    This changes the local habitat and the environment where they live.

gcsephysicsonline.com/**energy-resources**

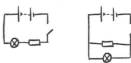

GCSE
DRAWING CIRCUITS

Circuit drawings are a simple way of displaying the workings of an electrical circuit, with each electrical component corresponding to its own symbol.

1. Sketch the circuit symbol for the following electrical components:

   a. A cell

   b. A wire

   c. A voltmeter

   d. An ammeter

   e. An open switch

   f. A filament lightbulb

   g. A resistor

   h. An LED

   i. A battery

2. Write down any pieces of equipment that would be useful in drawing circuit diagrams.

   Pencil and ruler.

3. Define the difference between a series circuit and a parallel circuit.

   A series circuit has multiple components on the same loop, a parallel circuit has multiple loops.

gcsephysicsonline.com/**circuits-symbols**

---

4. Name a component that must be connected in series and another that must be connected in parallel.

   An ammeter must be connected in series, a voltmeter must be connected in parallel.

5. Draw two different circuits that could both connect a bulb, a resistor and a switch to a battery.

6. Draw a parallel circuit with three loops, one loop with a switch and a bulb, another loop with an LED and a resistor and another with an ammeter and a variable resistor.

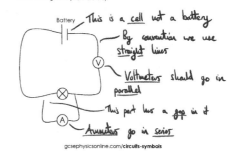

7. The circuit diagram below is both incorrect and badly drawn. Identify all the things that are wrong with it (there are five).

   This is a cell not a battery

   By convention we use straight lines

   Voltmeters should go in parallel

   This part has a gap in it

   Ammeters go in series

gcsephysicsonline.com/**circuits-symbols**

GCSE
CURRENT AND CHARGE

Current is the rate of flow of electric charge.

I = Q/t

1. Write down the equation using words rather than symbols and name the units that each of the three variables in the equation are measured in.

   A — $current = charge / time$ — C — s

2. i) Rearrange the equation to make **Q** the subject, then ii) rearrange to make **t** the subject.

   i) $Q = It$ ii) $t = \dfrac{Q}{I}$

3. In a circuit, charged particles flow through wires when a potential difference (voltage) is applied. Write down the name of these particles.

   Electrons

4. Conventional current flows in the opposite direction to these charged particles. Explain why. *Conventional current is from positive to negative, but electrons are negative so move to the positive terminal.*

5. Calculate the current when there is:

   a. 6.0 C of charge flowing past a point in a circuit over a period of 30 s

   $I = Q/t = 6.0/30 = 0.20\ A$ (2sf)

   b. 0.40 C of charge flowing past a point in a circuit over a period of 50 s

   $I = Q/t = 0.40/50 = 8.0 \times 10^{-3}\ A$ (or $8.0\ mA$)

   c. 36 C of charge flowing past a point in a circuit over a period of 3 minutes

   $I = Q/t = 36/(3\times60) = 0.20\ A$

6. Fill in the table with the missing values.

Current (A)	Charge (C)	Time (s)	Calculations
7.9	440	56	$Q = It = 7.9 \times 56 = 442.4$
0.12	430	3600	$Q = It = 0.12 \times 3600 = 432$
0.40	0.020	0.050	$t = Q/I = 0.020/0.40 = 0.05$
0.0030	6.3	2100	$t = Q/I = 6.3/0.0030 = 2100$

gcsephysicsonline.com/**current**

---

7. A student builds a simple electrical circuit. However, the reading on their ammeter is 0.0 A.

   a. Provided the ammeter isn't broken, write down a possible reason why the current might be zero

   It could have been connected in parallel.

   The issue is fixed. However, this time the reading on the ammeter is negative.

   b. Explain why this might be the case

   Because of the way the terminals are connected.

   The student rewires the circuit so that the ammeter reads a positive value of 1.4 A. The student disconnects the circuit after 25 s.

   c. Calculate the charge that has flowed through the ammeter

   $Q = It = 1.4 \times 25 = 35\ C$

   The student adds another power source such that the time it takes for the same amount of charge to flow through the circuit is 18 s.

   d. Calculate the reading that would display on the ammeter when the circuit was connected

   $I = \dfrac{Q}{t} = \dfrac{35}{18} = 1.944 \approx 1.9\ A$

8. A conventional oven requires a current of approximately 18 A. While cooking a meal, 32 400 C of charge is transferred through the oven.

   a. Calculate the time the oven takes to cook the meal

   $t = \dfrac{Q}{I} = \dfrac{32\,400}{18} = 1800\ s = 30\ minutes$

   For a different meal, the oven cooks it in 10 minutes less. ∴ 20 minutes

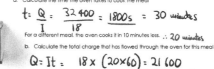

   b. Calculate the total charge that has flowed through the oven for this meal

   $Q = It = 18 \times (20\times60) = 21\,600 \approx 22\,000\ C$

9. In a small laptop, 450 mC is transferred through its circuit every minute.

   a. Calculate the current in the computer

   $I = \dfrac{Q}{t} = \dfrac{450\times10^{-3}}{60} = 7.5\times10^{-3}\ A$ ($7.5\ mA$)

   The battery in the laptop stores 135 C of charge.

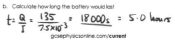

   b. Calculate how long the battery would last

   $t = \dfrac{Q}{I} = \dfrac{135}{7.5\times10^{-3}} = 18\,000\ s = 5.0\ hours$

gcsephysicsonline.com/**current**

GCSE
POTENTIAL DIFFERENCE, RESISTANCE AND CURRENT

The potential difference (or voltage) is a measure of how much energy the charged particles in a circuit have per unit charge. It is also related to current and resistance.

$$V = IR$$

1. Write down the equation using words rather than symbols and name the units that each of the three variables in the equation are measured in.

(voltage) potential difference = current × resistance
V   A   Ω

2. Ammeters are connected in series because they measure the current flowing through the circuit. Explain why voltmeters are connected in parallel.

To measure the electrical potential <u>across</u> a component.

3. i) Rearrange the equation to make I the subject. then ii) rearrange to make R the subject.

i) $I = \dfrac{V}{R}$ ii) $R = \dfrac{V}{I}$

4. Calculate the potential difference across:

a. A 4.0 Ω resistor with 2.5 A through it

$V = IR = 2.5 \times 4.0 = \underline{10\ V}$

b. A 7.5 Ω bulb with 0.20 A through it

$V = IR = 0.20 \times 7.5 = \underline{1.5\ V}$

c. A 1.4 kΩ resistor with 2.9 mA through it

$V = IR = 2.9 \times 10^{-3} \times 1.4 \times 10^{3} = 4.06$
$\approx \underline{4.1\ V}$ (2 sf)

5. Fill in the table with the missing values.

Voltage (V)	Current (A)	Resistance (Ω)	Calculations
12	30	0.40	$I = V/R = 12/0.40 = 30$
230	0.050	4600	$I = V/R = 230/4600 = 0.05$
9.0	0.30	30	$R = V/I = 9.0/0.30 = 30$
1.5	0.30	5.0	$R = V/I = 1.5/0.30 = 5$

2 sf

6. Mains electricity in your house has a potential difference of 230 V. A hairdryer, with a resistance of 46 Ω. is plugged in.

a. Calculate the current flowing through the hairdryer

$I = \dfrac{V}{R} = \dfrac{230}{46} = \underline{5.0\ A}$

A hair straightener is plugged into the same mains supply which causes a current of 2.3 A to flow.

b. Calculate the electrical resistance of the hair straighteners

$R = \dfrac{V}{I} = \dfrac{230}{2.3} = \underline{100\ Ω}$

7. A scientist builds a simple series circuit made of a 9.0 V battery and two resistors, R_1 and R_2. R_1 has a resistance equal to the hairdryer and R_2 has a resistance equal to the hair straighteners from the previous question. $R_1 = 46\ Ω$ $R_2 = 100\ Ω$

a. Draw the circuit and add one ammeter and two voltmeters in appropriate places

b. Calculate the current flowing through both R_1 and R_2 (2 sf)

$R_T = R_1 + R_2 = 46 + 100 = 146\ Ω$

$I = V/R = 9.0/146 = 0.06164 \approx \underline{0.062\ A}$

c. Calculate the potential difference across R_1 and potential difference across R_2

$V_1 = IR_1 = 0.06164 \times 46 = 2.836 \approx \underline{2.8\ V}$
$V_2 = IR_2 = 0.06164 \times 100 = 6.164 \approx \underline{6.2\ V}$
$(2.8 + 6.2 = 9.0\ V)$

8. A large lithium-ion battery holds 2.1 kC of charge. When connected in series to a 300 Ω resistor, the battery transfers all of its charge in exactly one day.

Calculate the potential difference across the battery

$I = \dfrac{Q}{t} = \dfrac{2100}{24 \times 60 \times 60} = 0.02431\ A$

$V = IR = 0.02431 \times 300 = 7.292$
$\approx \underline{7.3\ V}$ (2 sf)

GCSE
I-V CHARACTERISTICS

The I-V characteristics of an electrical component refer to the relationship between the current flowing through and the potential difference across the component.

1. Write down the equation for resistance in terms of current and potential difference (voltage).

$\text{resistance} = \dfrac{\text{potential difference}}{\text{current}}$

2. Define what an ohmic conductor is.

This is where (at a constant temperature) the <u>current</u> is <u>proportional</u> to the <u>potential difference</u>.

3. The graph on the right shows the I-V characteristics of two fixed resistors, A and B.

a. Write down if A is an ohmic conductor

Yes   (A has a straight line)

b. Explain which of the two resistors has a greater resistance and why

B. For the <u>same</u> value of V, the value of I is <u>less</u>, so the resistance must be greater.

4. A filament bulb is not an ohmic conductor. This means its resistance is not constant and hence its I-V graph is not a straight line.

a. Sketch the I-V graph for a filament bulb on the axes on the right

b. Describe in detail how a filament bulb produces light

The current causes the thin metal filament to heat up. It gets so hot it emits light.

c. Explain in detail why a filament bulb is not an ohmic conductor

Its resistance <u>changes</u>, so V not proportional to I.

5. A diode is unlike other electrical components for one main reason.

a. Write down what property makes a diode special

It only allows current to flow <u>one</u> way.

b. Sketch the I-V characteristic graph for a diode on the axes on the right

c. Write down what LED stands for

<u>Light emitting diode</u>

6. Below is a graph showing the relationship between the current through a resistor and the potential resistance across it. Calculate the resistance of the resistor.

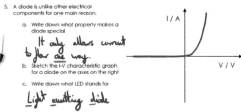

Read values off the graph

$R = \dfrac{V}{I}$

$R = \dfrac{1.0}{20}$

$R = 0.050\ Ω$

7. Below is a graph showing the relationship between the current through a different component and the potential resistance across it. Calculate the resistance of the bulb when the potential difference across it is -4.0 V.

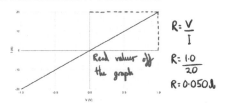

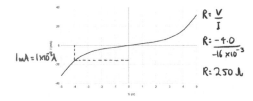

$1\ mA = 1 \times 10^{-3}\ A$

$R = \dfrac{V}{I}$

$R = \dfrac{-4.0}{-16 \times 10^{-3}}$

$R = 250\ Ω$

GCSE
LDRS AND THERMISTORS

LDRs and thermistors are both types of variable resistors. LDR is short for light dependent resistor - their resistance is dependent on light intensity whereas a thermistor's resistance is dependent on temperature.

1. Draw the symbols for i) an LDR and ii) a thermistor.

    i.   ii.

2. Describe the relationship between the resistance of an LDR and the light intensity.

As the light intensity _increases_ the resistance _decreases_.

3. Sketch and label a graph showing the relationship between the resistance of an LDR and light intensity on the axes below. Remember to label the axes.

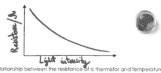

4. Describe the relationship between the resistance of a thermistor and temperature.

As the temperature _increases_ the resistance _decreases_.

5. Sketch a graph showing the relationship between the resistance of a thermistor and temperature on the axes below. Remember to label the axes.

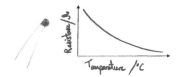

---

6. LDRs can be used in street lights as a sensor to turn the lights on and off. The diagram below shows a possible circuit set-up for a street light.

   a. Describe how the circuit on the right turns the street light on when it gets dark and turns it off when it gets light

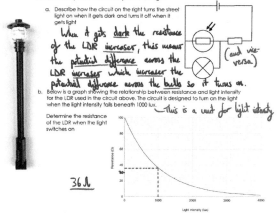

When it gets **dark** the resistance of the LDR **increases**, this means the potential difference across the LDR increases which increases the potential difference across the bulb so it turns on. (and vice versa)

   b. Below is a graph showing the relationship between resistance and light intensity for the LDR used in the circuit above. The circuit is designed to turn on the light when the light intensity falls beneath 1000 lux.

Determine the resistance of the LDR when the light switches on

this is a unit for light intensity

36 Ω

Thermistors can be used in a similar way but instead they can be used to sense when an object gets too hot or too cold. Below is a graph showing the relationship between resistance and temperature for a thermistor that is connected to a 9.0 V supply.

   c. Calculate the change in current flowing through the thermistor as the temperature is increased from 10 °C to 50 °C

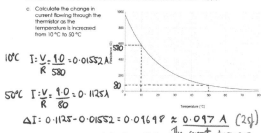

10°C $I = \dfrac{V}{R} = \dfrac{1.0}{580} = 0.01552\ A$

50°C $I = \dfrac{V}{R} = \dfrac{9.0}{80} = 0.1125\ A$

$\Delta I = 0.1125 - 0.01552 = 0.09698 \approx \underline{0.097\ A}$ (2sf)

The current increases

GCSE
SERIES CIRCUITS

Series circuits are when two or more electrical components are connected by wire to form a single conducting loop.

1. Identify the six circuit symbols drawn below.

Filament Bulb   Resistor   Voltmeter   Battery   Ammeter   Closed Switch

2. Identify any electrical components above that should only be connected in series.

The ammeter

3. Draw a circuit that has four 1.5 V cells connected to a diode, resistor and filament lamp in series. Include an ammeter that could be used to record the current through the resistor.

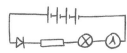

4. A simple series circuit is set up: a 6.0 V battery, a filament bulb and a resistor are connected in a single loop. The battery causes <u>72 C</u> of charge to flow through the circuit every minute.

   a. Draw a circuit diagram

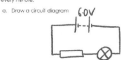

6·0V

   b. Calculate the current through the circuit

$I = \dfrac{Q}{t} = \dfrac{72}{60} = 1.2\ A$ (2sf)

The filament bulb has a resistance of 2.0 Ω and the resistor has a resistance of 3.0 Ω.

   c. Calculate the potential difference across:

      i. The filament bulb ← from part b.

$V = IR = 1.2 \times 2.0 = \underline{2.4V}$

      ii. The resistor

$V = IR = 1.2 \times 3.0 = \underline{3.6V}$

   d. Check the values of potential difference for the electrical components are correct by comparing them to the potential difference across the battery

$V_{++} + V_{\otimes} + V_{\square}$ $6.0 = 2.4 + 3.6$

   e. Calculate the total resistance of the circuit

$R_T = R_{\otimes} + R_{\square}$ or $R_T = \dfrac{V}{I} = \dfrac{6.0}{1.2} = \underline{5.0\ \Omega}$

$R_T = 2.0 + 3.0 = \underline{5.0\ \Omega}$

5. An <u>8.0 V</u> cell is connected in series to three identical resistors: $R_1 = R_2 = R_3 = \underline{3.0\ \Omega}$ and an ammeter.

   a. Calculate the total resistance of the circuit

8·0V

$R_T = R_1 + R_2 + R_3$

$R_T = 3.0 + 3.0 + 3.0$

$R_T = \underline{9.0\ \Omega}$

   b. Calculate the current flowing through every point in the circuit

$I = V/R_T = 8.0/9.0 = 0.8889 \approx \underline{0.89A}$ (2sf)

One of the resistors is removed and replaced by a 6.0 Ω resistor.

   c. Calculate the new current in the circuit $I = V/R_T = \dfrac{8.0}{12.0} = 0.6667$

$R_T = 3.0 + 3.0 + 6.0 = 12.0\ \Omega$ $\approx \underline{0.67A}$

   d. Compare the new current and resistance to the initial values

As the total resistance _increases_, the current _decreases_

$\dfrac{I_{new}}{I_{old}} = \dfrac{0.67}{0.89} = \dfrac{3}{4}$ $\dfrac{R_{new}}{R_{old}} = \dfrac{12}{9.0} = \dfrac{4}{3}$

GCSE
PARALLEL CIRCUITS

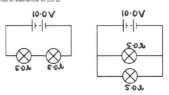

Parallel circuits occur when two or more electrical components are connected to form two or more conducting loops in a circuit.

1. State the effect on the overall resistance of adding a resistor in parallel to any circuit.

   The total resistance, R_T, decreases.

2. The current is the same everywhere in a parallel circuit (if false, explain).

   • True (False) *Could be a different value in each loop.*

3. In a parallel circuit, the potential difference across each loop is the same and equal to the potential difference across the cell or battery (if false, explain).

   (True) • False

4. Voltmeters must be connected to a circuit in parallel (if false, explain).

   (True) • False

5. A 10.0 Ω resistor and a filament bulb, with resistance 5.0 Ω, are connected in parallel to a 5.0 V cell.

   a. Draw the circuit.

   b. Write down the potential difference across both the resistor and the bulb

   Both 5.0V

   c. Calculate the current through i) the resistor and ii) the bulb

   i. $I = \dfrac{V}{R} = \dfrac{5.0}{10.0} = 0.50\ A$ (2sf)

   ii. $I = \dfrac{V}{R} = \dfrac{5.0}{5.0} = 1.0\ A$

   d. Hence calculate the total current flowing through the cell

   $I_T = 0.50 + 1.0 = 1.5\ A$

   e. Calculate the total resistance, R_T of the circuit

   $R_T = \dfrac{V}{I} = \dfrac{5.0}{1.5} = 3.333 \approx 3.3\ \Omega$

6. In both circuits below, the potential difference across the battery is 10.0 V and each bulb has a resistance of 5.0 Ω.

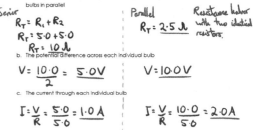

Calculate:

a. The total resistance of the bulbs in series and the combined resistance of the bulbs in parallel

Series
$R_T = R_1 + R_2$
$R_T = 5.0 + 5.0$
$R_T = 10\ \Omega$

Parallel
$R_T = 2.5\ \Omega$

Resistance halves with two identical resistors.

b. The potential difference across each individual bulb

$V = \dfrac{10.0}{2} = 5.0V$ $V = 10.0V$

c. The current through each individual bulb

$I = \dfrac{V}{R} = \dfrac{5.0}{5.0} = 1.0\ A$ $I = \dfrac{V}{R} = \dfrac{10.0}{5.0} = 2.0A$

d. Comment on the differences in the values of resistance, potential difference and current between the parallel and series circuits.

The series circuit has a higher total resistance and a lower potential difference and a smaller current through each lamp compared to the parallel circuit.

GCSE
SERIES AND PARALLEL CIRCUITS

Series and parallel circuits behave differently when we compare the current and potential difference in each part of the circuit.

1. Calculate the current at the points in the circuits below.

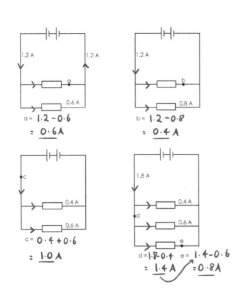

a = $1.2 - 0.6$
= $0.6 A$

b = $1.2 - 0.8$
= $0.4 A$

c = $0.4 + 0.6$
= $1.0 A$

d = $1.8 - 0.4$
= $1.4 A$ e = $1.4 - 0.6$
= $0.8 A$

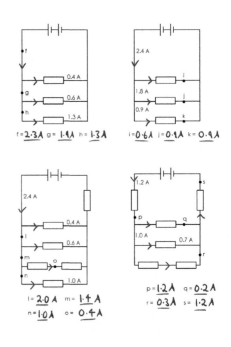

f = $2.3A$ g = $1.9A$ h = $1.3A$

i = $0.6A$ j = $0.9A$ k = $0.9A$

l = $2.0 A$ m = $1.4 A$
n = $1.0 A$ o = $0.4 A$

p = $1.2A$ q = $0.2A$
r = $0.3A$ s = $1.2A$

2. Calculate the potential difference (voltage) across each of these resistors in the circuits below.

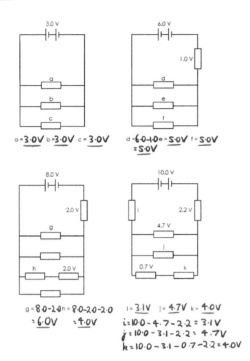

a = $3.0V$ b = $3.0V$ c = $3.0V$

d = $6.0-1.0$ e = $5.0V$ f = $5.0V$
= $5.0V$

g = $8.0-2.0$ h = $8.0-2.0-2.0$
= $6.0V$ = $4.0V$

i = $3.1V$ j = $4.7V$ k = $4.0V$

i = $10.0 - 4.7 - 2.2 = 3.1V$
j = $10.0 - 3.1 - 2.2 = 4.7V$
k = $10.0 - 3.1 - 0.7 - 2.2 = 4.0V$

3. Calculate the missing values in the circuits below.

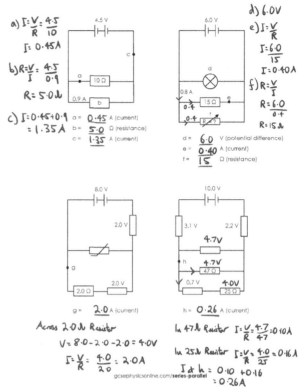

a) $I = \frac{V}{R} = \frac{4.5}{10}$

$I = 0.45A$

b) $R = \frac{V}{I} = \frac{4.5}{0.9}$

$R = 5.0\Omega$

c) $I = 0.45 + 0.9$
$= 1.35A$

a = $\underline{0.45}$ A (current)
b = $\underline{5.0}$ Ω (resistance)
c = $\underline{1.35}$ A (current)

d) $6.0V$

e) $I = \frac{V}{R}$

$I = \frac{6.0}{15}$

$I = 0.40A$

f) $R = \frac{V}{I}$

$R = \frac{6.0}{0.4}$

$R = 15\Omega$

d = $\underline{6.0}$ V (potential difference)
e = $\underline{0.40}$ A (current)
f = $\underline{15}$ Ω (resistance)

g = $\underline{2.0}$ A (current)

Across 2.0Ω Resistor
$V = 8.0 - 2.0 - 2.0 = 4.0V$
$I = \frac{V}{R} = \frac{4.0}{2.0} = 2.0A$

h = $\underline{0.26}$ A (current)

In 47Ω Resistor $I = \frac{V}{R} = \frac{4.7}{47} = 0.10A$

In 25Ω Resistor $I = \frac{V}{R} = \frac{4.0}{25} = 0.16A$

I at h = $0.10 + 0.16$
$= 0.26A$

GCSE
ELECTRICAL POWER

Both an increase in the current through a circuit and the potential difference across a circuit increase the rate of energy transfer. Hence they both increase the power of the circuit – the energy transferred per second.

$$P = VI$$

1. Write down the equation using words rather than symbols and name the units that each of the three variables in the equation are measured in.

$$\underset{W}{power} = \underset{V}{potential\ difference} \times \underset{A}{current}$$

2. Calculate the power when there is:

a. A current of 0.60 A and a potential difference of 12 V

$P = VI = 12 \times 0.60 = \underline{7.2 W}$

b. A potential difference of 0.20 V and a current of 800 mA

$P = VI = 0.20 \times 800 \times 10^{-3} = \underline{0.16 W}$

3. i) Rearrange the equation to make **V** the subject, then ii) rearrange to make I the subject.

i. $V = \frac{P}{I}$ ii. $I = \frac{P}{V}$

4. Write down the equation for potential difference in terms of current and resistance.

$V = IR$

5. Write down the equations for power in terms of i) potential difference and resistance, then ii) current and resistance.

i. $P = \frac{V^2}{R}$ ii. $P = I^2R$

6. Fill in the table with the missing values.

Power (W)	Voltage (V)	Current (A)	Calculations
1.2	80	0.015	$P = VI = 80 \times 0.015 = 1.2$
100	40	2.5	$V = P/I = 100/2.5 = 40$
12	10	1.2	$V = P/I = 12/1.2 = 10$
45	9.0	5.0	$I = P/V = 45/9.0 = 5$
8.2	12	0.68	$I = P/V = 8.2/12 = 0.6833$

(2✓)

7. A 150 W games console is plugged into a mains electricity supply at 230 V.

a. Calculate the current in through the console

$I = \frac{P}{V} = \frac{150}{230} = 0.6522 \approx \underline{0.652 A}$ (3 s.f.)

A student plays on the console for an hour and a half.

b. Calculate how much energy is transferred in this time

$E = Pt = 150 \times (90 \times 60) = \underline{810\ 000\ J}$

A portable console does not require mains electricity and only needs a fraction of the power. A lithium-ion battery produces a power of 12 W with a current of 1.6A.

c. Calculate the potential difference of the portable console's battery

$V = \frac{P}{I} = \frac{12}{1.6} = \underline{7.5V}$

8. For the circuit on the right, calculate the power dissipated by the:

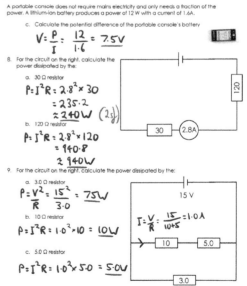

a. 30 Ω resistor

$P = I^2R = 2.8^2 \times 30$
$= 235.2$
$\approx \underline{240 W}$ (2 s.f.)

b. 120 Ω resistor

$P = I^2R = 2.8^2 \times 120$
$= 940.8$
$\approx \underline{940 W}$

9. For the circuit on the right, calculate the power dissipated by the:

a. 3.0 Ω resistor

$P = \frac{V^2}{R} = \frac{15^2}{3.0} = \underline{75W}$

b. 10 Ω resistor

$P = I^2R = 1.0^2 \times 10 = \underline{10W}$

$I = \frac{V}{R} = \frac{15}{10+5} = 1.0A$

c. 5.0 Ω resistor

$P = I^2R = 1.0^2 \times 5.0 = \underline{5.0W}$

We know that energy transferred is equal to the power multiplied by time.
However, energy transferred is also equal to voltage multiplied by charge.

energy transferred = total charge transferred x potential difference

1. Write down the equation using symbols rather than words and name the units that each of the three variables in the equation are measured in.

$$E = QV$$
$$J \quad C \quad V$$

2. Calculate the energy transferred when:

a. A 12 V potential difference that transfers a charge of 50 C

$$E = QV = 50 \times 12 = \underline{600 \ J}$$

b. A 2.2 kV potential difference that transfers a charge of 0.30 C

$$E = QV = 0.30 \times 2200 = \underline{660 \ J}$$ (2sf)

c. A 780 mV potential difference that transfers a charge of 3.2 kC

$$E = QV = 3.2 \times 10^3 \times 780 \times 10^3 = 2496 \approx \underline{2500 \ J}$$

3. i) Rearrange the equation to make **V** the subject, then ii) rearrange to make **Q** the subject.

i. $$V = \frac{E}{Q}$$ ii. $$Q = \frac{E}{V}$$

4. Use your equation for **V** to provide a definition of potential difference.

The potential difference is the energy transferred per unit charge.

5. Fill in the table with the missing values.

Energy (J)	Voltage (V)	Charge (Q)	Calculations
216	90.0	2.40	$E = QV = 2.40 \times 90.0 = 216$
656	8.20	80.0	$E = QV = 80.0 \times 8.20 = 656$
45 000	600	75	$Q = E/V = 45000/600 = 75$
450	60	7.5	$Q = E/V = 450/60 = 7.5$
0.0252	6.0	0.0042	$V = E/Q = 0.0252/0.0042 = 6$
7 200 000	800	9000	$V = E/Q = 7200000/9000 = 800$

3sf ← (rows 1,2) 2sf ← (rows 3,4) 1sf ← (row 6)

6. A kettle has a power rating of 2800 W and takes 3.0 minutes to boil exactly a litre of water.

a. Calculate how much energy is transferred to the water

$$E = Pt = 2800 \times (3 \times 60) = 504\ 000$$
$$\approx \underline{500 \ kJ} \quad (2sf)$$

The kettle is connected to mains electricity which has a potential difference of 230 V.

b. Calculate the total amount of charge transferred

$$Q = \frac{E}{V} = \frac{504\ 000}{230} = 2191 \approx \underline{2200 \ C} \quad (2sf)$$

A 60W light bulb is also connected to the mains and is left on for 5 hours.

c. Calculate if the bulb left on for 5 hours transfers more energy than the kettle does to boil **two** litres of water

Light bulb — $E = Pt = 60 \times (5 \times 60 \times 60) = \underline{1\ 080\ 000 \ J}$ The light bulb transfers more energy!

Kettle — $1\ ltr = 504\ 000 \ J$ ∴ $2\ ltrs = 1\ 008\ 000 \ J$

7. A single 6.0 V cell powers a handheld fan. When the weather is hot, 20 office workers each have an individual fan on for the whole working day which is 8 hours. The current drawn within a single fan is 0.15 A.

a. Calculate the energy transferred by the fans

one fan
$$Q = It = 0.15 \times (8 \times 60 \times 60) = 4320 C$$
$$E = QV = 20 \times 4320 \times 6.0 = 518400$$
number of fans $\approx \underline{520\ 000 \ J}$

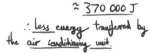

One of the workers suggests a small air conditioning unit for the whole office would be more efficient. A small air conditioning unit requires mains electricity and draws a current of 0.30 A but only needs to be on for a total of one and a half hours throughout the day to sufficiently cool the room.

b. Calculate if their claim is correct

Air conditioning unit ↓
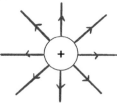

$$Q = It = 0.30 \times (90 \times 60) = 1620 C$$
$$E = QV = 1620 \times 230 = 372\ 600$$
$$\approx \underline{370\ 000 \ J}$$

∴ less energy transferred by the air conditioning unit.

Static electricity occurs when two objects have different charges, i.e. where one is positively charged and the other negatively charged.

1. Write down the relative charge of an electron.

−1 (Negative)

2. Explain why static electricity is more common between two insulators and not two conductors.

In a conductor the charged particles can move away. In an insulator they stay in the same place.

3. When two insulators are rubbed together, one loses some of its electrons to the other. Describe the effect this has on each individual insulator.

The insulator that loses electrons becomes positively charged, the insulator that gains electrons becomes negative.

4. Complete the following:

Like charges repel , opposite charges attract .

5. If one insulator gains electrons and the other loses them, write down if the two insulators attract or repel each other.

They attract one another.

6. Write down what surrounds every charged particle and how it might be displayed in a diagram.

There is an electric field, we can show this with electric field lines.

7. Describe how the direction of electric field lines are determined.

They point away from the positive charge.

8. Explain what it means when electric field lines are closer together.

This means the electric field there is stronger.

9. A circular balloon is rubbed on a woolly jumper. Draw the electric field lines around the balloon below.

10. A teacher rubs an inflated balloon on their head. The hair on the teacher's head loses electrons and the balloon gains them.

a. Write down which insulator is positively charged and which is negative

Hair — Positive
Balloon - Negative

b. Describe why the individual hairs on the teacher's head stand on end

All the hairs are positively charged, so they repel each other and spread apart as far as possible.

11. Static electricity occurs when charged particles collect on an insulator. The insulator is very bad at conducting electricity so the charged particles have nowhere to go.

a. Describe the dangers this may present

A large charge may build up, which could then cause an electric shock to a person or cause a spark.

b. Describe how you make an a highly charge insulator safe

You would 'earth' it, so there is no build up of charged particles.

GCSE
DENSITY

Density is a measure of the amount of stuff within a given space, more specifically the amount of mass.

$$\rho = m/V$$

This is the Greek letter 'rho'

1. Write down the equation using words rather than symbols.

density = mass/volume

2. Name the units that each of the three variables in the equation are measured in.

Sometimes g/cm³ is used — kg/m³   kg   m³

3. Calculate the density (in kg/m³) of:

a. A 690 kg object with a volume of 3.0 m³

$\rho = m/V = 690/3.0 = \underline{230 \ kg/m^3}$

b. A 270 kg mass with a volume of 0.090 m³

$\rho = m/V = 270/0.090 = \underline{3000 \ kg/m^3}$

c. A 7.8 kg mass with a volume of 480 cm³

$\rho = m/V = 7.8/480 \times 10^{-6} = 16250 \simeq \underline{16000 \ kg/m^3}$

4. Rearrange the original equation to make **m** the subject, then ii) rearrange to make **V** the subject.

i) $m = \rho V$ ii) $V = \dfrac{m}{\rho}$

5. Fill in the table with the missing values (to 2 sf).

Density [kg/m³]	Mass [kg]	Volume [m³]	Calculations
25	35.0	1.4	$\rho = m/V = 35.0/1.4 = 25$
1500	920	0.60	$\rho = m/V = 920/0.60 = 1533$
1000	10	0.010	$V = m/\rho = 10/1000 = 0.01$
8900	530	0.060	$V = m/\rho = 530/8900 = 0.05955$
1720	16	0.0093	$m = \rho V = 0.0093 \times 1720 = 15.996$
2300	460 000	200	$m = \rho V = 200 \times 2300 = 460 \ 000$

6. A swimming pool measures 25 m in length, 8.0 m in width and 1.2 m in depth.

a. Calculate the volume of the swimming pool

$V = 25 \times 8.0 \times 1.2 = \underline{240 \ m^3}$

Water has a density of ρ_{water} = 1000 kg/m³.

b. Calculate the mass of water inside the swimming pool

$m = \rho V = 1000 \times 240 = \underline{240 \ 000 \ kg}$

A heavy brick is often used for training purposes in the pool. A brick has dimensions of approximately 18 cm in length, 9.0 cm in height and 8.0 cm in depth and a density 1.9 times that of water.

c. Calculate the mass of the brick

$m = \rho V = (1.9 \times 1000) \times (0.18 \times 0.090 \times 0.080)$
$= 2.4624 \simeq \underline{2.5 \ kg}$ (2sf)

7. A box of cornflakes has a mass of 900 g and has side lengths of 40 cm, 25 cm and 10 cm.

Calculate the average density in kg/m³ of the cornflakes

$\rho = \dfrac{m}{V} = \dfrac{0.900}{0.40 \times 0.25 \times 0.10} = \underline{90 \ kg/m^3}$

8. Palladium has a density of approximately ρ = 12 g/cm³.

a. Calculate the volume in cm³ that 3.6 kg of palladium would take up

$V = \dfrac{m}{\rho} = \dfrac{3600 \ g}{12 \ g/cm^3} = \underline{300 \ cm^3}$

Palladium sells for £51 per gram.

b. Calculate the dimensions of a cube of palladium that costs £800 000

Calculate the mass $800000/51 = 15686.3 \ g$

$V = \dfrac{m}{\rho} = \dfrac{15686.3}{12} = 1307.2 \ cm^3$

volume of a cube of side x $V = x^3 \quad x = \sqrt[3]{V} = \sqrt[3]{1307.2} = 10.9 \simeq \underline{11 \ cm}$ (2sf)

GCSE
SPECIFIC HEAT CAPACITY 1

The specific heat capacity (shc) of a substance is the energy absorbed or released in order to raise or lower the temperature of 1 kg of that substance by 1 °C.

change in thermal energy = mass x specific heat capacity x change in temperature

1. Name the units that each of the four variables in the equation are measured in.

J   kg   J/kg°C   °C

2. Write down the equation using symbols rather than words.

θ= Greek letter 'theta' $\Delta E = mc\Delta\theta$ $\Delta Q = mc\Delta T$ Sometimes used as well

Δ= Greek letter 'delta' It means 'change in'

3. Calculate the change in thermal energy of:

a. A 4.0 kg mass with a specific heat capacity of 238 J/kg°C that has its temperature raised by 13 °C

$\Delta E = mc\Delta\theta = 4.0 \times 238 \times 13 = 12376 \simeq \underline{12000 \ J}$ (2sf)

b. A 0.30 kg mass with a specific heat capacity of 23 J/kg°C that has its temperature raised by 127 °C

$\Delta E = mc\Delta\theta = 0.30 \times 23 \times 127 = 876.3 \simeq \underline{880 \ J}$

4. i) Rearrange the equation to make **m** the subject. ii) rearrange to make **c** the subject and iii) rearrange to make **Δθ** the subject.

i) $m = \dfrac{\Delta E}{c\Delta\theta}$ ii) $c = \dfrac{\Delta E}{m\Delta\theta}$ iii) $\Delta\theta = \dfrac{\Delta E}{mc}$

5. Fill in the table with the missing values (to 2 sf).

ΔE [J]	m [kg]	c [J/kg°C]	Δθ [°C]	Calculations
67 000	3.2	4200	5.0	$3.2 \times 4200 \times 5.0 = 67200$
180 000	12	2100	7.1	$12 \times 2100 \times 7.1 = 178920$
4700	3.9	200	6.0	$4700/(3.9 \times 6.0) = 200.85$
1500	0.51	230	13	$1500/(0.51 \times 13) = 226.24$
820	0.069	1200	9.9	$820/(1200 \times 9.9) = 0.06902$
28	3.8×10^{-3}	230	32	$28/(230 \times 32) = 3.804 \times 10^{-3}$
1700	0.026	1000	65	$1700/(0.026 \times 1000) = 65.385$

6. A puddle of water has a mass of 5.0 kg and a temperature of 15 °C. In the evening, the puddle's temperature drops to 3.0 °C. c_{water} = 4200 J/kg°C

a. Calculate the change in energy, if we assume no water is lost to evaporation

$\Delta E = mc\Delta\theta = 5.0 \times 4200 \times (15 - 3.0)$
$= 252 \ 000 \simeq \underline{250 \ 000 \ J}$ (2sf)

A student claims that if the temperature were to drop by half the amount, the change in energy would also be half.

b. Use calculations to back up the student's claim

Originally $\Delta\theta$ = 12°C , now $\Delta\theta$ = 6°C

$\Delta E = mc\Delta\theta = 5.0 \times 4200 \times 6 = 126 \ 000 \ J = $ half the original value

The student is correct

It rains overnight, causing the mass of the puddle to increase. The next evening, the puddle's temperature drops from 15 °C to 3.0 °C but the change in energy is 30% greater than in part a.

c. Calculate the mass of the water puddle

$\Delta\theta = 12°C \quad c = 4200 \quad \Delta E = 1.3 \times 252000 = 327600$

$m = \Delta E / c\Delta\theta = \dfrac{327600}{4200 \times 12} = \underline{6.5 \ kg}$

7. A scientist spills 0.72 kg of liquid mercury onto the floor. Whilst the scientist goes to get equipment to clean it up, the liquid warms by 3.0 °C. $c_{mercury}$ = 126 J/kg°C

a. Calculate the change in energy

$\Delta E = mc\Delta\theta = 0.72 \times 126 \times 3.0 = 272.16$
$\simeq \underline{270 \ J}$ (2sf)

The scientist wants to compare an unknown liquid to mercury. They pour 0.72 kg of the new liquid on the floor. Its change in energy is the same as the mercury in part a, but its temperature rises by 6.3 °C.

b. Calculate the unknown liquid's specific heat capacity

$c = \dfrac{\Delta E}{m\Delta\theta} = \dfrac{272.16}{0.72 \times 6.3} = \underline{60 \ J/kg°C}$

8. Aluminium has a specific heat capacity 900 J/kg°C and a density 2.72 g/cm³.   not needed for this question!

280 g of aluminium is heated from an initial temperature of 15°C so that it absorbs 3820 J of energy.

Calculate its final temperature

$\Delta\theta = \dfrac{\Delta E}{mc} = \dfrac{3820}{0.280 \times 900} = 15.16 \simeq 15°C$ (2sf)

Final temp = Original temp + $\Delta\theta$ = 15 + 15 = $\underline{30°C}$

GCSE
SPECIFIC HEAT CAPACITY 2

The equation for the change in energy of an object involving the specific heat capacity can be written using symbols as:

$$\Delta E = mc\Delta\theta$$

1. A kettle can heat a maximum of 1.5 kg of water to boiling. A scientist fills the kettle up fully with water at 15 °C. c_{water} = 4.2 kJ/kg°C

   a. Calculate the energy needed to boil the kettle of water (assuming it is 100% efficient)

   water boils at 100°C

   $$\Delta E = mc\Delta\theta = 1.5 \times 4200 \times (100-15) = 535\,500$$
   $$\doteqdot 540\,000 \text{ J} \quad (2sf)$$

   convert from 4.2 kJ/kg°C

   The scientist wants to use 20% less energy when boiling the kettle. They decide to boil less water, again starting at 15 °C.

   b. Calculate the mass of water needed to transfer 20% less energy

   $$\Delta E \propto m \quad (c \text{ and } \Delta\theta \text{ are constant})$$

   $$m = \frac{1.5}{1.2} = 1.25 \text{ kg}$$

   The scientist hears that milk has a specific heat capacity of 3.93 kJ/kg°C.

   c. Calculate how much energy it would take to raise 2 pints of milk to 100 °C if it was initially in a fridge at 4.0 °C
   (1 pint = 568 ml and the density of milk is similar to water)

   $$\Delta E = mc\Delta\theta = (2 \times 0.568) \times 3930 \times (100-40)$$
   $$(1000\text{ml} = 1\text{ kg}) \qquad = 428510 \doteqdot 430\,000 \text{ J}$$

   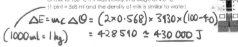

2. A 0.70 kg block of copper is heated using a 150 W heater. In one and a half minutes, the copper block's temperature has been raised from 12 °C to 63 °C.

   Calculate the specific heat capacity of copper.

   $$E = Pt = 150 \times 90 = 13500 \text{ J}$$

   convert to seconds

   $$c = \frac{\Delta E}{m\Delta\theta} = \frac{13500}{0.70 \times (63-51)} = 378.15$$
   $$\doteqdot 380 \text{ J/kg°C}$$
   $$(2sf)$$

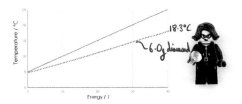

18.3°C

6.0 g diamond

3. The graph above shows how the energy supplied to a massive 4.0 g diamond changes its temperature. The diamond starts at 5.0 °C and is carefully supplied with a total of 40 J of energy.

   a. Calculate the specific heat capacity of diamond

   data taken from the graph

   $$c = \frac{\Delta E}{m\Delta\theta} = \frac{40}{4.0 \times 10^3 \times (25-5)} = 500 \text{ J/kg°C}$$

   b. Describe how the graph would look if a 6.0 g diamond was tested, again starting at 5.0 °C and supplied with 40 J of energy

   The graph would be a straight line starting at 5°C, but would have a lower gradient

4. Lithium has one of the highest specific heat capacities of any metal. A large 2300 g block of lithium is heated from 20 °C, such that it absorbs 503 kJ. $c_{lithium}$ = 3560 J/kg°C

   a. Calculate the lithium block's final temperature

   $$\Delta\theta = \frac{\Delta E}{mc} = \frac{503\,000}{2.300 \times 3560} = 61.43 \doteqdot 61°C \quad \theta_{final} = 20 + 61 = 81°C$$
   $$(2sf)$$

   b. If the same amount of energy had been transferred to the same mass of water at 20 °C, calculate final temperature of the water and compare this to the value for lithium

   $$\Delta\theta = \frac{\Delta E}{mc} = \frac{503\,000}{2.300 \times 4200} = 52.07 \doteqdot 52°C$$
   $$\theta_{final} = 72°C$$

   This is a lower final temperature - water has a very high shc value

---

GCSE
SPECIFIC LATENT HEAT

The specific latent heat of a substance is the energy released or absorbed in order to change the state of 1 kg of that substance without changing the temperature.

energy required for a change of state = mass x specific latent heat

1. Name the units that each of the three variables in the equation are measured in.

   J   kg   J/kg

2. Write down the equation using symbols rather than words.

   $$\Delta E = mL$$

3. Calculate the energy needed to change the state of the following.
   L_{water} (solid to liquid) = 334 kJ/kg L_{water} (liquid to gas) = 2260 kJ/kg.

   a. 2.1 kg of water into water vapour

   $$\Delta E = mL = 2.1 \times 2260000 = 4746000$$
   $$\doteqdot 4\,700\,000 \text{ J}$$

   b. 350 g of ice into water

   $$\Delta E = mL = 0.350 \times 334000 = 116\,900 \doteqdot 120\,000 \text{ J}$$

4. i) Rearrange the equation to make **m** the subject then ii) rearrange to make **L** the subject.

   i) $$m = \frac{\Delta E}{L}$$ ii) $$L = \frac{\Delta E}{m}$$

5. Fill in the table with the missing values (to 2 sf).

E (J)	m (kg)	L (J/kg)	Calculations
1 200 000	3.4	340 000	$\Delta E = mL = 3.4 \times 340000 = 1\,156\,000$
12 000 000	59	210 000	$\Delta E = mL = 59 \times 210000 = 12\,390\,000$
25 000	0.011	2 300 000	$L = \Delta E/m = 25000/0.011 = 2\,272\,727$
8 900	0.040	220 000	$L = \Delta E/m = 8900/0.040 = 222\,500$
59 000	0.30	200 000	$m = \Delta E/L = 59000/200000 = 0.295$
42 000	0.091	460 000	$m = \Delta E/L = 42000/460000 = 0.0913$

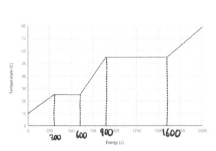

6. The graph shows what happens to the temperature of an unknown substance when energy is supplied. The substance has a mass of 2.5 kg.

   a. From the graph, calculate the substance's specific latent heat of fusion (solid to liquid) and vaporisation (liquid to gas)

   fusion $$L_f = \frac{\Delta E}{m} = \frac{600-300}{2.5} = 120 \text{ J/kg}$$

   vaporisation $$L_v = \frac{\Delta E}{m} = \frac{1600-900}{2.5} = 280 \text{ J/kg}$$

   The mass of the substance is changed such that 40% more energy is needed to change it from a solid to a liquid.

   b. Calculate the new mass of the substance

   $$\Delta E \propto m \qquad m = 2.5 \times 1.4 = 3.5 \text{ kg}$$

   Increase ΔE by 40% because m increases by 40% as well

7. Water has different values of specific latent heat for different transitions:

   L (solid to liquid) = 334 kJ/kg
   L (liquid to gas) = 2260 kJ/kg
   c_{water} = 4200 J/kg°C

   Calculate how much thermal energy is required to fully change 370g of ice at 0°C into water vapour.

   Melting $$\Delta E = mL_f = 0.370 \times 334 \times 10^3 = 123\,580$$

   Heating $$\Delta E = mc\Delta\theta = 0.370 \times 4200 \times 100 = 155\,400$$

   Boiling $$\Delta E = mL_v = 0.370 \times 2260 \times 10^3 = 836\,200$$

   $$\text{Total } \Delta E = 1\,115\,180 \doteqdot 1\,120\,000 \text{ J}$$
   $$1.12 \text{ MJ}$$

GCSE
ATOMS AND ISOTOPES

Atoms make up everything you see around you. Atomic elements are defined by their number of protons whereas isotopes of elements have a different number of neutrons.

1. Write down the relative charges of the proton, electron and neutron.

   +1 (proton), -1 (electron) and 0 (neutron)

2. Write down where the majority of an atom's mass is and what particles it contains.

   In the nucleus, this contains protons and neutrons.

3. Write down where you would find the electrons in an atom.

   They would be orbiting the nucleus in shells.

4. Describe what happens when an electron in an atom a) loses energy and b) gains energy.

   a. It moves to a lower shell, at its lowest energy level & is in its 'ground state'.

   b. The electron can jump to a higher energy level.

5. Explain the role electrons in the outer shell have in the behaviour of an element (GCSE Chemistry style question).

   Atoms like to have a full outer shell.

6. Define the atomic number of an element.

   The number of protons in the nucleus.

7. Define the mass number of an element.

   The total number of protons AND neutrons in the nucleus.

8. Write down how we use the symbols of a chemical element: and its mass and atomic numbers to represent elements.

   mass no. — A
   atomic no. — Z   X — chemical symbol

9. Elements are neutrally charged. Write down what this tells us about the numbers of electrons, protons and neutrons within the atom.

   The number of protons EQUALS the number of electrons in an atom.

10. Write down the definition of an 'isotope'.

    An element with a different number of neutrons in the nucleus.

11. The number of protons, electrons and neutrons in an atom is always a whole number (an integer). Explain why an element's mass number is not always a whole number on the periodic table.

    The mass number in the periodic table is often an average value of the isotopes of that element.

12. Describe how you would work out the number of neutrons in an element if you know its atomic and mass numbers.

    Mass number minus the atomic number.

13. Define the term 'ion'.

    A charged atom.

14. Describe J.J. Thomson's plum pudding model.

    Protons and electrons distributed throughout the atom.

15. Explain the results of the alpha-scattering experiment and what this proves about the structure of the atom.

    Most of the alpha particles passed straight through — so the atom is largely empty space.

    Some of the positive alpha particles were deflected by more than 90° — so the dense core must have a positive charge.

GCSE
RADIOACTIVE DECAY

Unstable nuclei emit either particles or electromagnetic radiation to become more stable. This is called radioactive decay.

1. Name the three most common types of radiation, and their symbols, that are released when a nucleus decays.

   Alpha α, beta β and gamma γ.

2. Write down i) what an alpha particle is made of and ii) what a beta particle is made of.

   i) Two protons and two neutrons   ii) An electron

3. Fill in the table.

Type of radiation	Alpha (α)	Beta (β)	Gamma (γ)
Charge	+2	-1	neutral
Relative mass	4	$\frac{1}{2000}$	0
Object that stops the radiation	Paper, skin	3mm Aluminium	Thick Lead
Does the radiation change the element?	Changes to a different element	Changes to a different element	Stays the same element

4. Define the atomic number of an element and write down its symbol.

   The number of protons in the nucleus, Z.

5. Define the mass number of an element and write down its symbol.

   The total number of protons AND neutrons in the nucleus, A.

6. Write down what happens to an element's atomic number if it undergoes i) alpha emission, ii) beta emission and iii) gamma emission.

   i) Decreases by 2   ii) Increases by 1   iii) Nothing

7. Write down what happens to an element's mass number if it undergoes i) alpha emission, ii) beta emission and iii) gamma emission.

   i) Decreases by 4   ii) Nothing   iii) Nothing

8. Describe the process that allows beta decay to take place. Think about how a negatively charged particle can be emitted from a nucleus that only contains positive and neutral particles (protons and neutrons).

   A neutron turns into a proton and an electron.
   neutral → positive + negative

9. Fill in the boxes to complete the general nuclear equation describing alpha emission for an element, X, decaying into element Y.

   $$^A_Z X \rightarrow ^{A-4}_{Z-2} Y + ^4_2 \alpha \quad \left(or \; ^4_2 He \right)$$

10. Complete the nuclear equation for radon undergoing alpha decay.

    $$^{226}_{88} Ra \rightarrow ^{222}_{86} Rn + ^4_2 \alpha$$

11. Fill in the boxes to complete the general nuclear equation describing beta emission for an element, X, decaying into element Z.

    $$^A_Z X \rightarrow ^A_{Z+1} Z + ^0_{-1} \beta \quad \left(or \; ^0_{-1} e \right)$$

12. Complete the nuclear equation for carbon undergoing beta decay.

    $$^{14}_6 C \rightarrow ^{14}_7 N + ^0_{-1} \beta$$

13. Write down the general nuclear equation for an element, X, undergoing gamma decay.

    $$^A_Z X \rightarrow ^A_Z X + ^0_0 \gamma$$

14. Write down the nuclear equation for cobalt-60 undergoing gamma decay. Cobalt has an atomic number, Z = 27.

    $$^{60}_{27} Co \rightarrow ^{60}_{27} Co + ^0_0 \gamma$$

15. Write down if the following decays are possible and if they are, name the process of decay (you may need a periodic table to help you).

    a. Thorium-232 can decay to radium-228
       Yes - alpha $^{232}_{90} Th \rightarrow ^{228}_{88} Ra + ^4_2 \alpha$
    b. Carbon-14 can decay into oxygen-14
       Not possible
    c. Uranium-238 can decay to thorium-232
       Not possible
    d. Technetium-99 can decay into technetium-99
       Yes - gamma $^{11}_{43} Tc \rightarrow ^{11}_{43} Tc + ^0_0 \gamma$
    e. Lithium-8 can decay into beryllium-8
       Yes - beta $^8_3 Li \rightarrow ^8_4 Be + ^0_{-1} \beta$

GCSE
HALF-LIFE

A sample of radioactive nuclei will decay exponentially. This means that the number of nuclei of the original element will decrease by the same proportion for each time period of the same length. The time for a sample to halve is its half-life.

1. Write down the unit for activity.

    B_q

2. Define the half-life of an element in terms of its activity.

    The time it takes for the activity of a radioactive isotope to fall to half of its initial activity.

3. State if the following are examples of exponential decay:

    a. The number of original nuclei of an element halves after 10 s, halves again after another 10 s and halves again after another 10 s

    Yes

    b. The activity of an element halves after 10 s, halves again after another 20 s and halves again after another 30 s

    No

    c. The activity of an element reduces by a third after one minute, reduces by a third again after another minute and reduces by a third again after another minute

    Yes

Half-lives	Proportion
0	1
1	½
2	¼
3	⅛
4	1/16
5	1/32

4. Complete the following:

    a. After 1 half-life, the activity is ½ the original value

    b. After 2 half-lives, the activity 1/4 the original value

    c. After 4 half-lives, the activity 1/16 the original value

    d. After 5 half-lives, the activity is 1/32 the original value

5. A sample of an element has an initial activity of 3.00×10^{11} Bq. Calculate the activity after:

    a. One half-life

    $3.00 \times 10^{11} \times \frac{1}{2} = \underline{1.50 \times 10^{11}}$ Bq

    b. Three half-lives

    $3.00 \times 10^{11} \times \frac{1}{8} = \underline{3.75 \times 10^{10}}$ Bq   (3sf)

6. Nobelium-259 has a half-life of 58 minutes. A sample is measured as having an initial activity of 8.00×10^8 Bq.

    a. Calculate the estimated activity of the sample after three half-lives

    $\frac{1}{8} \times 8.00 \times 10^8 = \underline{1.00 \times 10^8}$ Bq

    b. Calculate the estimated activity of the sample after 4 hours and 50 minutes

    $4:50 = 5$ half-lives $\therefore \frac{1}{32} \times 8.00 \times 10^8 = \underline{2.50 \times 10^7}$ Bq

    After some time has passed, the activity of the sample is measured at 6.25×10^6 Bq.

    c. Calculate how much time has passed since the original measurement

    $\frac{6.25 \times 10^6}{8.00 \times 10^8} = \frac{1}{128}$ $\therefore \frac{1}{128}$ of the initial activity = 7 half-lives

    $7 \times 58 = 406$ minutes (6 hours 46 min)

7. Carbon-14 is a radioactive isotope that has a half-life of 5730 years and is used in carbon dating. The remains of an archaeological specimen is tested. a sample containing carbon-14 is estimated to have an activity that is 3.125 % of its original value.

    Calculate the approximate age of the bones.

    $3.125\% = \frac{1}{32} = 5$ half-lives

    $5 \times 5730 = 28650$

    ≈ 29 thousand years

8. A sample of fermium-253 has an initial activity of 6.4×10^{10} Bq. After 12 days, the activity falls to 4.0×10^9 Bq.

    a. Calculate the half-life of fermium-253

    $\frac{4.0 \times 10^9}{6.4 \times 10^{10}} = \frac{1}{16}$ $\therefore 4$ half-lives in 12 days

    1 half-life = 3 days

    b. Calculate the estimated activity of the sample 3 weeks after the initial measurement

    3 weeks = 21 days = 7 half-lives

    $\frac{1}{128} \times 6.4 \times 10^{10} = \underline{5.0 \times 10^8}$ Bq

GCSE
FISSION AND FUSION

Fission occurs when a heavy nucleus splits whereas fusion occurs when two light nuclei join together.

1. Write down two types of heavy isotopes that are commonly used in nuclear reactors for nuclear **fission**.

    Uranium-235 and plutonium-239

2. Write down the name given to the two smaller nuclei that are produced from fission.

    Daughter products

3. Write down what else is released from nuclear fission.

    Neutrons

4. Describe how the fission of one nucleus can lead to a chain reaction and potentially an explosion.

    A neutron emitted in one reaction could be absorbed by another U-235 nucleus - or many more!

5. Write down the famous equation that describes the amount of energy released from the nucleus in a nuclear reaction.

    $E = mc^2$

6. Briefly describe how electricity is produced by a nuclear power station, starting with the fission of radioactive nuclei.

    A uranium-235 nucleus absorbs a neutron. This splits apart releasing two smaller isotopes and 2 or 3 neutrons (which cause further fission reactions). The kinetic energy stored in these particles is transferred to the thermal store of the reactor. This heats up water until it turns to steam. This turns turbines which turns a generator.

7. Describe how the rate of reaction in a nuclear power station can be increased or decreased.

    Control rods absorb neutrons. By adjusting their position the rate of reaction can be controlled.

8. Explain the problems spent fuel rods present to the environment.

    The daughter products remain radioactive for hundreds of thousands of years.

9. Describe some benefits of nuclear fission compared to fossil fuel power stations.

    No greenhouse gases are emitted.

10. Write down where in the Universe you would find nuclear **fusion** occurring naturally.

    Inside the core of stars.

11. Write down the particle(s) within a hydrogen nucleus.

    A proton.

12. Write down the particle(s) within a helium nucleus.

    Two protons and two neutrons.

13. Two hydrogen nuclei can fuse together, forming a deuterium nucleus. However, deuterium nuclei contain one proton and one neutron, so explain what must have happened in this reaction.

    A proton has changed into a neutron.

14. A deuterium nucleus fuses together with another hydrogen nucleus (none of the protons or neutrons change in this reaction). Write down the number of protons and neutrons in the resulting particle and the element it is an isotope of.

    Two protons and one neutron. It is an isotope of helium. $^{3}_{2}He$

15. The particle in question 14 can fuse with another of the same particle to produce a helium nucleus with two protons and two neutrons. Write down the particles that must be ejected when this occurs.

    Two protons are ejected $\left(^{3}_{2}He + ^{3}_{2}He \rightarrow ^{4}_{2}He + 2 \, ^{0}_{1}p \right)$

16. Write down the problems scientists currently face making nuclear fusion a viable energy source on Earth.

    The process is very unstable and it takes more energy to make it happen than is given out.

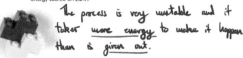

GCSE
IDENTIFYING FORCES

Force is a vector quantity, meaning that it has size and direction. There are many different forces that exist in the world around us.

1. Write down the unit that force is measured in.

N (newton)

2. Explain the difference between contact and non-contact forces.

Non-contact forces act at a distance.

3. Give some examples of a) contact forces and b) non-contact forces.

a. Friction, normal contact force, upthrust and drag

b. Gravitational, magnetic and electrostatic

4. Many people use the terms mass and weight to mean the same thing, when in fact the mass and weight of an object are different.

a. Define the meaning of weight

The force on a mass due to a gravitational field.

b. Describe the differences between mass and weight

Mass is the same anywhere in the Universe, weight is the force acting on the mass.

c. Write down the formula for weight in both symbols and words

W = mg   weight = mass × gravitational field strength

d. Write down the value of the gravitational field strength on (or very near to) the surface of Earth

9.8 N/kg (Sometimes 10 N/kg used at GCSE)
9.81 Nkg⁻¹ is used at A Level)

5. Explain how friction is caused.

By the interaction between two surfaces.

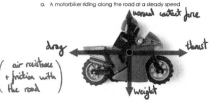

6. Explain why seemingly smooth surfaces still cause friction.

When you look really closely they are not perfectly smooth. ——— small bumps

7. Describe how a lubricant reduces friction between two surfaces.

This separates the two surfaces so they can slide over one another with less force.

8. Explain how a fluid produces drag on a solid object.

This is caused by the solid object colliding with particles in the gas/liquid.

9. Identify the forces acting on the following objects:

a. A motorbiker riding along the road at a steady speed

normal contact force
drag   thrust
(air resistance + friction with the road)
weight

b. A swimmer floating in the sea

upthrust
weight

c. A rugby ball that is at the highest point in its flight path after it has been kicked (moving to the right)

drag (air resistance)
weight

GCSE
FREE BODY DIAGRAMS

Free body, or force, diagrams are a simple way of displaying the forces acting on an object.

1. Name the four main forces acting on a car, travelling at constant velocity.

Thrust, drag, weight and the normal contact force

normal contact force
drag ← → thrust
weight

On the left is a force diagram of the car in question 1.

a. Describe what the black dot represents

The car.

b. Match each of the four forces to an arrow

2. Describe the resultant force acting on an object if it is at rest or travelling at a constant velocity.

The resultant force is equal to zero.

3. Describe the resultant force acting on an object that is accelerating or decelerating.

There is now a resultant force acting on the object.

4. If two forces are acting on an object in the same direction, describe how we could display this on a force diagram.

We would add the arrows end to end.

5. Explain how we display the size of the forces acting on an object on a free body diagram.

The length of the arrow is proportional to the size.

6. The force diagram on the left shows the forces acting on a different car moving from left to right.

a. Describe the motion of the car

The car is accelerating to the right.

The driver of the car (on the previous page) puts the car in neutral and slams on the brakes, i.e. there is no forward force.

b. Draw a diagram showing the forces acting on the car, a second after braking.

normal contact force
drag + braking force ←
weight

7. a. Draw a free body diagram showing the forces acting on a homemade rocket a split second after taking off. There is a slight wind blowing from left to right.

thrust
→ force due to the wind
weight

b. Draw a free body diagram showing the forces acting on the same rocket after some time has passed and is decelerating i.e. the upward forces are less than the downward forces. The wind blowing from left to right has increased.

thrust
→ force due to the wind
weight
drag

8. a. Draw a free body diagram showing the forces acting on a monkey that is hanging from a branch by its tail.

normal contact force
weight

b. Describe how the diagram would differ if it showed the monkey leaping midway between two trees and explain what this tells you about the motion of the monkey.

The weight downwards would be the same size and direction. There would be no normal contact force (and a small amount of drag) so the monkey would accelerate.

GCSE
RESOLVING FORCES

The force acting on an object at an angle can be resolved into two or more components, usually the horizontal and vertical components. Forces can be resolved either mathematically or graphically (by scale drawing).

1. Write down Pythagoras's theorem for right angled triangles.

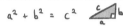

$$a^2 + b^2 = c^2$$

2. Write down the three trigonometric identities that are in SOH-CAH-TOA.

$$\sin\theta = \frac{O}{H} \qquad \cos\theta = \frac{A}{H} \qquad \tan\theta = \frac{O}{A}$$

3. If a force acts on an object at an angle, it can be resolved into horizontal and vertical components. For the following four questions, resolve the force into its two components.

   a. Resolve a single force of 6.0 N acting at 45° to the horizontal.

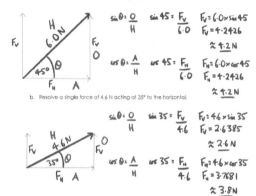

$$\sin\theta = \frac{O}{H} \qquad \sin 45 = \frac{F_v}{6.0} \qquad F_v = 6.0 \times \sin 45$$
$$F_v = 4.2426$$
$$\approx \underline{4.2\,N}$$

$$\cos\theta = \frac{A}{H} \qquad \cos 45 = \frac{F_H}{6.0} \qquad F_H = 6.0 \times \cos 45$$
$$F_H = 4.2426$$
$$\approx \underline{4.2\,N}$$

   b. Resolve a single force of 4.6 N acting at 35° to the horizontal.

$$\sin\theta = \frac{O}{H} \qquad \sin 35 = \frac{F_v}{4.6} \qquad F_v = 4.6 \times \sin 35$$
$$F_v = 2.6385$$
$$\approx \underline{2.6\,N}$$

$$\cos\theta = \frac{A}{H} \qquad \cos 35 = \frac{F_H}{4.6} \qquad F_H = 4.6 \times \cos 35$$
$$F_H = 3.7681$$
$$\approx \underline{3.8\,N}$$

   c. Resolve a single force of 3.7 N acting at 70° to the horizontal.

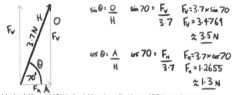

$$\sin\theta = \frac{O}{H} \qquad \sin 70 = \frac{F_v}{3.7} \qquad F_v = 3.7 \times \sin 70$$
$$F_v = 3.4769$$
$$\approx \underline{3.5\,N}$$

$$\cos\theta = \frac{A}{H} \qquad \cos 70 = \frac{F_H}{3.7} \qquad F_H = 3.7 \times \cos 70$$
$$F_H = 1.2655$$
$$\approx \underline{1.3\,N}$$

4. A horizontal force of 4.3 N to the right and a vertical force of 3.2 N up act on an object. Find the resultant force acting on the object.

(This is adding vectors)

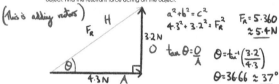

$$a^2 + b^2 = c^2 \qquad F_R = 5.360$$
$$4.3^2 + 3.2^2 = F_R^2 \qquad \approx \underline{5.4\,N}$$

$$\tan\theta = \frac{O}{A} \qquad \theta = \tan^{-1}\left(\frac{3.2}{4.3}\right)$$
$$\theta = 36.66 \approx \underline{37°}$$

5. An explorer pulls a sled behind her by a rope that ties around her waist. She pulls the sled with a force of 230 N at an angle of 43.8° above the ground.

   Resolve the tension in the rope using a mathematical method.

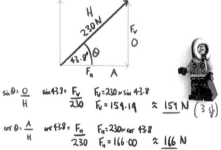

$$\sin\theta = \frac{O}{H} \qquad \sin 43.8 = \frac{F_v}{230} \qquad F_v = 230 \times \sin 43.8$$
$$F_v = 159.19 \qquad \approx \underline{159\,N} \;(3\,sf)$$

$$\cos\theta = \frac{A}{H} \qquad \cos 43.8 = \frac{F_H}{230} \qquad F_H = 230 \times \cos 43.8$$
$$F_H = 166.00 \qquad \approx \underline{166\,N}$$

GCSE
WORK DONE

Mechanical work done is the name we give to the energy transferred by a force to move an object with mass a certain distance.

work done = force × distance

1. Write down the equation using symbols rather than words and name the units that each of the three variables in the equation are measured in.

$$W = Fs$$
$$\;\;\; J \quad N \quad m$$

2. Explain the relationship between the direction of the force and the distance travelled.

It is the distance travelled in the direction of the force.

3. Calculate the work done by:

   a. A 25 N force acting over a distance of 6.0 m

$$W = Fs = 25 \times 6.0 = \underline{150\,J} \qquad (2\,sf)$$

   b. A 0.45 N force acting over a distance of 10 cm

$$W = Fs = 0.45 \times 0.10 = \underline{0.045\,J}$$

   c. A 100 kN force acting over 5.3 km

$$W = Fs = 100 \times 10^3 \times 5.3 \times 10^3 = \underline{5.3 \times 10^8\,J}$$

4. i) Rearrange the original equation to make **F** the subject, then ii) make **s** the subject.

   i) $$F = \frac{W}{s}$$
   ii) $$s = \frac{W}{F}$$

5. Fill in the table with the missing values.

	Work done (J)	Force (N)	Distance (m)	Calculations
3 sf	812000	912	890	$W = Fs = 912 \times 890 = 811680$
2 sf	87	52	1.7	$s = W/F = 87/52 = 1.67$
	7900	0.70	11 000	$s = W/F = 7900/0.70 = 11286$
3 sf	670	39.4	17.0	$F = W/s = 670/17.0 = 39.412$
2 sf	90	7.5	12	$F = W/s = 90/12 = 7.5$

6. A school janitor pulls his cart full of cleaning supplies along with a constant force of 89 N against friction.

   a. Calculate the work done by the janitor as he pulls the cart along a 28 m hallway

$$W = Fs = 89 \times 28 = 2492 \approx \underline{2500\,J} \qquad (2\,sf)$$

Throughout the day, as the janitor uses up his cleaning products, the cart's mass decreases. By the end of the day the janitor needs to apply a force that is 25% less than at the start.

   b. Calculate the work done by the janitor as he pulls the cart at the end of the day along the same hallway

$$W = 2492 \times 0.75 = 1869 \approx \underline{1900\,J}$$
25% less ↑

The janitor uses a mop bucket to clean up some mess. He drags the mop with a force of 17 N across the floor.

   c. Calculate the distance, in the direction of the force, covered by the mop head as he does 850 J of work.

$$s = \frac{W}{F} = \frac{850}{17} = \underline{50\,m}$$

7. A lift in a hospital, which itself has a mass of 250 kg, has a maximum capacity of 700 kg. Some doctors and nurses get in the lift such that the lift is at 80% capacity.

   a. Calculate the work done by the lift as it carries the medical staff up 3 floors (each floor is 2.4 m high)

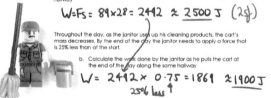

$$m = 250 + (0.80 \times 700) = 810\,kg$$
$$F = \text{weight} = mg = 810 \times 9.8 = 7938\,N$$
$$W = Fs = 7938 \times (3 \times 2.4) = 57154 \approx \underline{57\,000\,J} \;(2\,sf)$$

The lift is used to transport a heavy piece of medical equipment, that has a mass of 540 kg, to a higher floor by two hospital workers that have an average mass of 80 kg. The work done by the lift is 111 720 J.

   b. Calculate how many floors up the lift carries the workers and the equipment

$$m = 250 + 540 + 80 + 80 = 950\,kg$$
$$F = \text{weight} = mg = 950 \times 9.8 = 9310\,N$$
$$s = \frac{W}{F} = \frac{111\,720}{9310} = 12\,m$$
$$12/2.4 = 5 \;\therefore\; \underline{5\,floors}$$

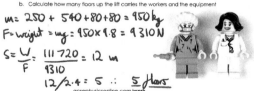

Springs store elastic potential energy if they are either extended or compressed. How much a spring is extended or compressed, by a certain force, is dependent on its spring constant.

F = ke (it can also be written as **F = kx** or **F = kΔl**)

1. Write down the equation using words rather than symbols and name the units that each of the three variables in the equation are measured in.

force = spring constant × extension
N   N/m   m

2. Define the extension of a spring.

The change in length.

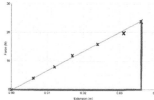

3. Calculate the force acting on a spring with:

a. A spring constant of 80 N/m that is extended by 0.25 m

F = ke = 80 × 0.25 = 20N   (2 ✓)

b. A spring constant of 0.50 N/m that is extended by 700 mm

F = ke = 0.50 × 0.700 = 0.35 N

4. i) Rearrange the equation to make **k** the subject, then ii) rearrange to make **e** the subject.

i) $k = \dfrac{F}{e}$ ii) $e = \dfrac{F}{k}$

5. Fill in the table with the missing values.

Force (N)	Spring constant (N/m)	Extension (m)	Calculations
0.36	0.40	0.90	F = ke = 0.40 × 0.90 = 0.36
6.5	18	0.36	F = ke = 18 × 0.36 = 6.48
12	20	0.60	k = F/e = 12/0.60 = 20
25	500	0.050	k = F/e = 25/0.050 = 500
1.0	7.4	0.14	e = F/k = 1.0/7.4 = 0.1351
8.5	90	0.094	e = F/k = 8.5/90 = 0.0944

(2 ✓)

6. Write down how you would describe the behaviour of a material that has been:

a. stretched beyond the limit of proportionality, so that it cannot return to its original shape

Plastic behaviour

b. stretched within the limit of proportionality, so that it returns to its original shape

Elastic behaviour

7. State Hooke's Law.

The force is proportional to the extension - provided it has not gone beyond the limit of proportionality.

8. A 7.0 cm long stretchy spring has a spring constant of approximately 16 N/m.

a. Calculate the **total** length of the spring if a force of 5.4 N acts to stretch it

$e = \dfrac{F}{k} = \dfrac{5.4}{16} = 0.3375$ $l = 0.070 + 0.3375 = 0.4075$

≈ 41 cm   (2 ✓)

The spring is hung on a hook and a mass is hung on the bottom.

b. Calculate the mass needed to extend the band by 1.2 cm

$F = ke = 16 \times 0.012 = 0.192$ N $m = \dfrac{W}{g} = \dfrac{0.192}{9.8} = 0.0196$ ≈ 0.020 kg

9. A student wants to test the properties of a spring they found. They hang a mass on the spring and measure the results, which are in the table below.

a. Complete the table below on the left by calculating the force applied on the spring by the mass (use g = 10 N/kg) and plot your results on the axes on the right

Mass (kg)	Extension (m)	Force (N)
0	0	0.0
0.4	0.006	4.0
0.8	0.012	8.0
1.2	0.017	12
1.6	0.024	16
2.0	0.031	20
2.4	0.036	24

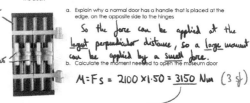

b. Calculate the gradient of the graph and explain what this represents

gradient = $\dfrac{\Delta y}{\Delta x} = \dfrac{24}{0.036} = 666.7 \approx 670$ (2 ✓) = spring constant

k = 670 N/m

A moment is the turning effect caused by applying a force at a distance from the pivot point (or turning point).

moment = force × distance

1. Name the units that each of the three variables in the equation are measured in.

Nm   N   m

2. Describe the relationship between the direction of the force and the distance to the turning point.

It is the perpendicular distance from the force applied to the turning point.

3. Calculate the moment of:

a. A 45 N force acting at a perpendicular distance of 4.0 m

M = Fs = 45 × 4.0 = 180 Nm

b. A 9.0 N force acting at a perpendicular distance of 70 cm

M = Fs = 9.0 × 0.70 = 6.3 Nm

4. i) Rearrange the equation to make **force** the subject, then ii) rearrange to make **distance** the subject.

i) $F = \dfrac{M}{s}$ ii) $s = \dfrac{M}{F}$

5. Fill in the table with the missing values.

Moment (Nm)	Force (N)	Distance (m)	Calculations
8.0	0.40	20	M = Fs = 0.40 × 20 = 8
195	780	0.250	M = Fs = 780 × 0.250 = 195
52.2	90.0	0.580	s = M/F = 52.2/90.0 = 0.58
800	160	5.00	s = M/F = 800/160 = 5
1.4	28	0.050	F = M/s = 1.4/0.050 = 28
270	41.5	6.50	F = M/s = 270/6.50 = 41.538

2 ✓
3 ✓
2 ✓
3 ✓

6. Some students go to visit a museum. One of the exhibits is an incredibly heavy door with several door handles attached at different points. A worker explains that a force of 2.10 kN at a perpendicular distance of 1.50 m from the hinges is needed to open the door.

a. Explain why a normal door has a handle that is placed at the edge, on the opposite side to the hinges

So the force can be applied at the largest perpendicular distance, so a large moment can be applied by a small force.

door
handles

b. Calculate the moment needed to open the museum door

M = Fs = 2100 × 1.50 = 3150 Nm   (3 ✓)

None of the students can open the door on their own but the two strongest, Celine and Noah, can pull the door if they work together. Noah pulls on one handle with a force of 1.20 kN at a perpendicular distance of 1.40 m.

c. Calculate the moment produced by Noah

M = Fs = 1200 × 1.40 = 1680 Nm

Celine pulls with a force of 1.40 kN.

d. Calculate the perpendicular distance from the hinges to the handle Celine is pulling on

$M_{open} = M_{Noah} + M_{Celine}$

$3150 = 1680 + (1400 \times s)$ $s = \dfrac{1470}{1400} = 1.05$ m (3 ✓)

Four other students try pulling on the door. Beth pulls with a force of 900 N at a distance of 60.0 cm, Nicole pulls with a force of 1.20 kN at a distance of 80.0 cm, Rachel pulls with a force of 800 N at a distance of 30.0 cm and Yasmine pulls with an unknown force at a distance of 1.25 m.

e. Calculate the force that Yasmine applies on her handle if they just manage to open the door

$M_{open} = M_{Beth} + M_{Nicole} + M_{Rachel} + M_{Yasmine}$

$3150 = (900 \times 0.600) + (1200 \times 0.800) + (800 \times 0.300) + (F \times 1.25)$

F = 1128 $\approx$ 1130 N   (3 ✓)

The pressure acting on the surface of a solid is the force applied per unit area.

pressure = force/area

1. Write down the equation using symbols rather than words and name the units that each of the three variables in the equation are measured in, including two different units for pressure.

$$N/m^2 \text{ or } Pa \qquad p = \frac{F}{A} \quad \begin{matrix}N\\m^2\end{matrix}$$

2. Write down the approximate value of atmospheric pressure on Earth at sea level.

$$\approx 101\,000 \text{ Pa}$$

3. Calculate the pressure caused by:

   a. A 120 N force acting over an area of 1.2 m²

$$p = F/A = 120/1.2 = \underline{100 \text{ Pa}}$$

   b. A 380 N force acting over an area of 0.250 m²

$$p = F/A = 380/0.250 = \underline{1520 \text{ Pa}}$$

   c. A 1.7 kN force acting over 0.0017 m²

$$p = F/A = 1700/0.0017 = \underline{1\,000\,000 \text{ Pa}}$$

4. i) Rearrange the original equation to make F the subject, then ii) rearrange to make A the subject.

  i) $$F = pA$$
  ii) $$A = \frac{F}{p}$$

5. Fill in the table with the missing values.

Pressure (Pa)	Force (N)	Area (m²)	Calculations
0.0600	12.0	200	p=F/A = 12.0/200 = 0.06
101 000	101 000	1.00	A=F/p=101000/101000=1
43 000	86 000	2.0	A=F/p = 86000/43000 = 2
22.8	0.114	0.00500	F=pA = 22.8×0.00500=0.114
700	47 600	68.0	F=pA = 700×68.0 = 47600

6. The atmospheric pressure at sea-level on Earth is 101 kPa. Because everything around us is at the same pressure we don't notice it. The surface area of a human varies between approximately 0.25 m² for a newborn baby to 1.8 m² for the average adult.

  a. Calculate the force from the atmosphere acting on a newborn baby

$$F = pA = 101\,000 \times 0.25 = 25\,250$$
$$\approx \underline{25 \text{ kN}} \quad (2sf)$$

  b. Calculate the force from the atmosphere acting on an average adult

$$F = pA = 101\,000 \times 1.8 = 181\,800$$
$$\approx \underline{180 \text{ kN}} \quad (2sf)$$

The force acting on a football pitch due to air pressure is 707 MN. The pitch is 100 m long.

  c. Calculate the area of a football pitch and its width

$$A = \frac{F}{p} = \frac{707\times10^6}{101\,000} = 7000\,m^2 \qquad \text{width} = 7000 \div 100$$
$$= \underline{70 \text{ m}}$$

7. A science lab wants to test the strength of a sheet of metal to see how it deforms. A sample is cut out and suspended by its four corners. **Ignore** the effect of air pressure in your calculations.

A square weight, with mass 110 kg and sides of 10 cm, is placed on the metal sheet.

  a. Calculate the pressure caused by the weight on the metal

$$F = W = mg = 110 \times 9.8 = 1078N \qquad p = \frac{F}{A} = \frac{1078}{0.010} = 107800$$
$$A = 0.10 \times 0.10 = 0.010\,m^2 \qquad\qquad \approx 110 \text{ kPa}$$

The metal does not bend so a different weight is used. A rectangular block, with a mass of 150 kg, is placed on the metal. The surface in contact with the sheet measures 20 cm x 5.0 cm.

  b. Calculate the pressure caused by this weight on the metal

$$F = W = mg = 150 \times 9.8 = 1470N \qquad p = \frac{F}{A} = \frac{1470}{0.010} = 147\,000$$
$$A = 0.20 \times 0.050 = 0.010\,m^2 \qquad\qquad \approx \underline{150 \text{ kPa}} \quad (2sf)$$

Still the metal does not bend. The scientists balance a small metal cone of mass 18 kg whose pointed end bends the metal sheet, leaving behind an indentation.

  c. Without using calculations, explain why the cone is able to bend the sheet even though the mass is much smaller

Although the force applied is small the area in contact is really small, so a large pressure is applied.

The pressure acting on an object submerged in a fluid is dependent on the height of fluid above it, the density of the fluid and the gravitational field strength.

pressure = height of fluid x density of fluid x gravitational field strength

1. Write down the equation using symbols rather than words and name the units that each of the four variables in the equation are measured in, including two different units for pressure.

$$N/m^2 \text{ or } Pa \qquad p = h\rho g \qquad \begin{matrix}m \quad kg/m^3 \quad N/kg\end{matrix}$$

2. Calculate the increase in pressure (from atmospheric pressure) at a depth of:

  a. 2.9 m deep in a pool of water (ρ_{water} = 1 000 kg/m³)

$$p = h\rho g = 2.9 \times 1000 \times 9.8 = 28420 \approx \underline{28 \text{ kPa}} \quad (2sf)$$

  b. 8.0 km under the ocean's surface ($\rho_{deep\,ocean}$ = 1 060 kg/m³)

$$p = h\rho g = 8000 \times 1060 \times 9.8 = 83\,104\,000 \approx \underline{83 \text{ MPa}}$$

  c. 30 cm deep in a tank of liquid mercury ($\rho_{mercury}$ = 13 700 kg/m³)

$$p = h\rho g = 0.30 \times 13700 \times 9.8 = 40278 \approx \underline{40 \text{ kPa}}$$

3. Rearrange the equation to make i) h the subject, ii) ρ the subject and iii) g the subject

  i) $$h = \frac{p}{\rho g}$$
  ii) $$\rho = \frac{p}{hg}$$
  iii) $$g = \frac{p}{h\rho}$$

4. Fill in the table with the missing values. (g = gravitational field strength.)

Pressure (kPa)	Height (m)	g (N/kg)	Density (kg/m³)	Calculations
101	3.40	9.80	3030	ρ=p/hg =101000/3.40×9.80 = 3031.2
700	90.0	6.80	1140	ρ=p/hg =700000/90.0×6.80= 1143.8
101	10.3	9.80	1 000	h=p/ρg =101000/1000×9.80 = 10.306
150	19.1	9.80	800	h=p/ρg =150000/800×9.80 = 19.133
101	10.2	7.50	1320	g=p/hρ =101000/10.2×1320 = 7.5015
5.30	3.10	1.88	909	g=p/hρ =5300/3.10×909 = 1.8808

5. An Olympic diver diving off a 10 m high platform into a pool can go as deep as 3.5 m.

  a. Calculate the **increase** in pressure acting on the diver at this depth

$$\rho_{water} = 1\,000 \text{ kg/m}^3$$
$$p = h\rho g = 3.5 \times 1000 \times 9.8$$
$$= 34300 \approx \underline{34 \text{ kPa}} \quad (2sf)$$

  b. Calculate the depth at which the **total** pressure acting on the diver is 150 kPa

change in pressure due to water   atmospheric pressure

$$\Delta p = 150\,000 - 101\,000 = 49\,000 \text{ Pa}$$
$$h = \frac{p}{\rho g} = \frac{49000}{1000 \times 9.8} = \underline{5.0 \text{ m}}$$

In an alternate reality, diving competitions are held on the moon in an artificial atmosphere that is at the same pressure as Earth's atmosphere. The gravitational field strength on the moon is about 1/6 of the value as Earth's gravitational field strength.

  c. Calculate the increase in pressure acting on a diver underwater at a depth of 2.0 m

$$p = h\rho g = 2.0 \times 1000 \times \left(\frac{1}{6} \times 9.8\right) = 3266.7$$
$$\approx \underline{3.3 \text{ kPa}}$$
$$\therefore \rho = 1000 \text{ kg/m}^3$$

6. A deep-sea diver trains in a deep freshwater tank. They need to be able to withstand a **total** pressure that is 2.5 times that of atmospheric pressure.

Calculate how deep they would need to dive to experience this.

$$\Delta p = 1.5 \times \text{atmospheric pressure}$$
$$= 1.5 \times 101\,000 = 151\,500 \text{ Pa}$$
$$h = p/\rho g = 151500/1000 \times 9.8 = 15.459 \approx \underline{15 \text{ m}}$$

7. The method of calculating pressure in fluids can be applied to calculate an approximate value of atmospheric pressure as well. After all, air is a fluid.

  a. Write down the value of atmospheric pressure at sea-level

$$\underline{101\,000 \text{ Pa}}$$

The atmosphere is estimated to be approximately 100 km high.

  b. Calculate the **average** density of the atmosphere, assuming that **g** is constant (please note that the average density is much less dense than the density at sea-level and that g is slightly weaker 100 km above the surface)

$$\rho = \frac{p}{hg} = \frac{101\,000}{100\,000 \times 9.8} = 0.10306$$
$$\approx \underline{0.10 \text{ kg/m}^3} \quad (2sf)$$

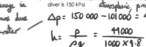

GCSE SPEED

Speed is a measure of how quickly an object is travelling.

$$v = s/t$$

1. Write down the equation using words rather than symbols and name the units that each of the three variables in the equation are measured in.

$$\text{m/s} \quad speed = \frac{distance}{time} \quad \begin{array}{c} m \\ s \end{array}$$

2. Calculate the speed of an object that travels:
   a. 500 m in 10 s

   $$v = s/t = 500/10 = \underline{50 \text{ m/s}} \quad (2 \text{ sf})$$

   b. 9.0 km in one minute

   $$v = s/t = 9000/60 = \underline{150 \text{ m/s}}$$

   c. 0.80 cm in 4.0 s

   $$v = s/t = 0.80 \times 10^{-3}/4.0 = \underline{2.0 \times 10^{-3} \text{ m/s}}$$

3. Write down or calculate:
   a. How many seconds are in one hour $\quad 60 \times 60 = \underline{3600 \text{ s}}$
   b. How fast 1.0 m/s is in miles per hour (1 mile ≈ 1600 m)

   $$1.0 \text{ m/s} = 3600 \text{ m/hour} \div 1600 = 2.25 \approx \underline{2.3 \text{ mph}} \ (2 \text{ sf})$$

4. i) Rearrange the equation to make s the subject, then ii) rearrange to make t the subject.

   i) $\quad s = vt$
   ii) $\quad t = \dfrac{s}{v}$

5. Fill in the table with the missing values.

Speed (m/s)	Distance (m)	Time (s)	Calculations
10	9000	900	$s = vt = 10 \times 900 = 9000$
3.00	108 000	3600	$s = vt = 3.00 \times 3600 = 10\,800$
0.89	890	1000	$t = s/v = 890/0.89 = 1000$
12	852	71	$t = s/v = 852/12 = 71$

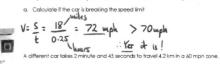

6. Average speed cameras are used to enforce different speed limit zones on the motorway. A car takes exactly 15 minutes to cover 18 miles in a 70 mph zone.

   a. Calculate if the car is breaking the speed limit

   $$v = \frac{s}{t} = \frac{18 \text{ miles}}{0.25 \text{ hours}} = \boxed{72 \text{ mph}} > 70 \text{ mph} \quad \therefore \text{ Yes it is!}$$

   A different car takes 2 minute and 45 seconds to travel 4.2 km in a 60 mph zone.

   b. Calculate if this car is breaking the speed limit (60 mph ≈ 27 m/s)

   $$v = \frac{s}{t} = \frac{4200 \text{ m}}{165 \text{ s}} = 25.45 \text{ m/s} < 27 \text{ m/s} \quad \therefore \underline{No} \text{ it isn't}$$

   A lorry is limited to a top speed of 90 km/h.

   c. Calculate its top speed in m/s

   $$90 \text{ km/h} = 90\,000 \text{ m/h} \div 3600 = \underline{25 \text{ m/s}}$$

   The same lorry enters a 60 mph zone that is 4.6 miles long. The driver wants to know how long it will take him to travel the length of the 60 mph zone.

   d. Calculate how much time the lorry would take to travel the 4.6 miles

   $$1 \text{ mile} = 1600 \text{ m} \quad \therefore \ 4.6 \text{ miles} = 4.6 \times 1600 = 7360 \text{ m}$$

   $$t = s/v = 7360/25 = 294.4 \text{ s} \approx \underline{4 \text{ min } 54 \text{ seconds}}$$

   The lorry is 22.5m long. The driver thinks to himself that it would take him a quarter of an hour, travelling at max speed, to cover a thousand lorry-lengths.

   e. Calculate whether or not the driver is correct

   $$v_{max} = 25 \text{ m/s}$$

   $$t = \tfrac{1}{4} \text{ hour} = 15 \times 60 = 900 \text{ s}$$

   $$s = v_{max} t = 25 \times 900 = \underline{22\,500 \text{ m}}$$

   $$22\,500 \div 22.5 = 1000$$

   $\underbrace{22\,500}_{\text{distance travelled}} \div \underbrace{22.5}_{\text{lorry length}} = 1000 \quad \therefore$ Yes, the driver is correct

GCSE VELOCITY

Velocity is the speed of an object in a given direction.

$$v = s/t$$

1. Write down the equation for velocity using words rather than symbols and name the units that each of the three variables in the equation are measured in.

$$\text{m/s} \quad velocity = \frac{displacement}{time} \quad \begin{array}{c} m \\ s \end{array}$$

2. Speed and distance are examples of which type of quantity:

   A scalar quantity.

3. Velocity and displacement are examples of:

   A vector quantity.

4. Describe the difference between distance and displacement.

   Distance is a scalar quantity, but displacement is the distance in a certain direction.

5. Describe the difference between speed and velocity.

   Speed is the distance travelled per unit time, but velocity is the rate of change of displacement.

6. Calculate the average velocity of:
   a. A car that is displaced 640 m in 40 s

   $$v = s/t = 640/40 = \underline{16 \text{ m/s}} \quad (2 \text{ sf})$$

   b. A tennis ball that is displaced 12 m in 0.80 s

   $$v = s/t = 12/0.80 = \underline{15 \text{ m/s}}$$

   c. A toy train that travels 80cm forwards then 30cm backwards in 10 s

   $$v = s/t = (0.80 - 0.30)/10 = \underline{0.050 \text{ m/s}}$$

   d. An Olympic swimmer who swims 100 m in a 50 m pool in 48 s

   $$v = s/t = 0/48 = \underline{0 \text{ m/s}}$$

7. A wildlife photographer sets out to find some crocodiles. She drives her 4x4 for 45 minutes on a perfectly straight road and covers 35 miles (1 mile ≈ 1600 m).

   a. Calculate the explorer's velocity in m/s

   $$v = \frac{s}{t} = \frac{35 \times 1600}{45 \times 60} = 20.74 \approx \underline{21 \text{ m/s}} \ (2 \text{ sf})$$

   The photographer sees some crocodiles in a lake. The crocodiles' swimming speed is measured at 4.0 m/s.

   b. Calculate how long a crocodile would take to cross the 48 m wide lake if it swam directly from shore to shore

   $$t = \frac{s}{v} = \frac{48}{4.0} = \underline{12 \text{ s}}$$

   A crocodile swims at a constant speed of 4.0 m/s from shore to shore but takes 24 s to do so.

   c. Explain how this can be the case and include a calculation for the velocity of the crocodile

   $$v = \frac{s}{t} = \frac{48}{24} = \underline{2.0 \text{ m/s}} \quad \text{It doesn't swim in a straight line.}$$

   One crocodile starts to chase the photographer on land! She zig-zags as she runs so that the crocodile has to zig-zag as well, slowing it down. Her car is 80 m away but they cover a distance of 240 m.

   d. Calculate the ratio between the explorer's speed and their velocity

   $$\frac{\text{Speed}}{\text{velocity}} = \frac{distance/t}{displacement/t} = \frac{240}{80} = \underline{3:1}$$

   The photographer drives straight home in a panic and gets into bed.

   e. Calculate the average velocity of the photographer from the moment she wakes up in bed in the morning to when she gets back into bed in the evening

   $$s = 0 \text{ and } v = \frac{s}{t} \quad \therefore \ v = \underline{0 \text{ m/s}}$$

8. The Earth travels around the Sun in a circular orbit with a radius of approximately 1.5×10^{11} m. As we know, the Earth takes 365.25 days to complete an orbit.

   Calculate the average velocity of the Earth as it completes exactly half an orbit.

   $$v = \frac{s}{t} = \frac{2r}{\tfrac{1}{2}T} = \frac{2 \times 1.5 \times 10^{11}}{\tfrac{1}{2} \times 365.25 \times 24 \times 60 \times 60} = 19\,013$$

   $$\approx \underline{19\,000 \text{ m/s}}$$

GCSE
ACCELERATION

Acceleration is the rate of change of an object's velocity with respect to time. In other words, it is a measure of how quickly the velocity of an object changes.

acceleration = change in velocity/time

1. Name the units that each of the variables in the equation are measured in.

m/s^2 m/s s

2. Write down the equation using symbols rather than words.

$$a = \frac{\Delta v}{t} \quad or \quad a = \frac{v-u}{t}$$

3. Calculate the acceleration of:

a. An object going from rest to 14 m/s in 10 s

$$a = \frac{v-u}{t} = \frac{14-0}{10} = 1.4 \, m/s^2$$

b. An object decelerating from 100 m/s to 5.0 m/s in 38s

$$a = \frac{v-u}{t} = \frac{5.0-100}{38} = -2.5 \, m/s^2$$

$(2\cancel{f})$

c. An object accelerating from rest to 120 m/s in one and a half minutes

$$a = \frac{v-u}{t} = \frac{120-0}{90} = 1.333 \approx 1.3 \, m/s^2$$

4. i) Rearrange the equation to make **v** the subject, ii) rearrange to make **u** the subject and iii) rearrange to make **t** the subject.

i) $v = u + at$ ii) $u = v - at$ iii) $t = \frac{v-u}{a}$

5. Fill in the table with the missing values.

a (m/s²)	v (m/s)	u (m/s)	t (s)	Calculations
3.0	140	5.0	45.0	$v = u + at = 5.0 + (3 \times 45) = 140$
24.0	84.8	12.8	3.00	$v = u + at = 12.8 + (24 \times 3) = 84.8$
11.1	66.9	44.7	2.00	$u = v - at = 66.9 - (11.1 \times 2) = 44.7$
10	136	16	12	$u = v - at = 136 - (10 \times 12) = 16$
135	36.5	23.0	0.100	$t = v - u/a = (36.5 - 23)/135 = 0.1$
1.4	423.3	3.5	300	$t = v - u/a = (423.3 - 3.5)/1.4 = 299.86$

6. Ironman decides to test how fast he can accelerate vertically upwards. He starts from the ground, at rest, and gets to a velocity of 230 m/s in 12 s.

a. Calculate Ironman's acceleration

$$a = \frac{v-u}{t} = \frac{230-0}{12} = 19.17 \approx 19 \, m/s^2 \, (2\cancel{f})$$

b. If Ironman were to change direction, whilst travelling at a constant 230 m/s, explain whether he would be accelerating or not

Yes, because as he changes direction his velocity changes

After making some adjustments, Ironman repeats his test. This time he gets to a velocity of 260 m/s but it takes him 14 s.

c. Determine if Ironman's acceleration has improved

$$a = \frac{v-u}{t} = \frac{260-0}{14} = 18.57 < 19.17$$

No it hasn't

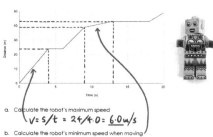

7. A teacher attaches a gas cylinder to a wheelie bin. She opens the cylinder, releasing the gas, which accelerates the bin at a constant rate of 1.2 m/s². The bin reaches a final velocity of 23 m/s.

a. Calculate the time the bin takes to accelerate to 23 m/s

$$t = \frac{v-u}{a} = \frac{23-0}{1.2} = 19.17 \approx 19 \, s \, (2\cancel{f})$$

She wants to increase the bin's final velocity. She pushes the bin so that it's travelling at an initial velocity of 3.6 m/s. The acceleration is still 1.2 m/s².

b. Calculate the final velocity after 20 s

$$v = u + at = 3.6 + (1.2 \times 20) = 27.6 \approx 28 \, m/s$$

Still unhappy with the bin's final velocity, she tweaks the gas cylinder such that the acceleration is increased to 1.5 m/s². However, this means the cylinder can only accelerate the bin for 15 s. She pushes the bin at an initial velocity of 4.7 m/s.

c. Calculate if the bin reaches a final velocity greater than in part b.

$$v = u + at = 4.7 + (1.5 \times 15) = 27.2 \approx 27 \, m/s$$
$$27.2 < 27.6 \therefore lower \, velocity$$

d. Calculate how fast the bin would have to be initially travelling for the bin to reach 30 m/s in 15 s

$$u = v - at = 30 - (1.5 \times 15) = 7.5 \, m/s$$

GCSE
DISTANCE-TIME GRAPHS

Distance-time graphs show us how far an object travels within a certain time. They can also be used to work out the speed of an object.

1. Write down the units for speed and hence the equation for speed.

m/s speed = distance / time

2. Below is a simple distance-time graph for an object. Calculate the following:

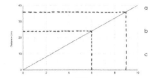

a. The distance travelled after 6 s

24m

b. The time it takes to travel 36 m

9.0 s

c. The speed of the object

$$v = \frac{s}{t} = \frac{40}{10} = 4.0 \, m/s$$

3. Below is a distance-time graph for a mountain-biker. Calculate the speed:

a. In the first 6 seconds

$$v = \frac{s}{t} = \frac{18}{6.0} = 3.0 \, m/s$$

b. Between 6 and 10 seconds

$$v = 0 \, m/s$$

c. Between 10 and 15 seconds

$$v = \frac{s}{t} = \frac{10}{5.0} = 2.0 \, m/s$$

Using the graph, write down:

d. The total distance covered

28m

e. The total time taken

15 s

f. Hence, calculate the average speed of the mountain-biker

$$v = \frac{s}{t} = \frac{28}{15} = 1.8667 \approx 1.9 \, m/s$$

4. This is a distance-time graph showing the movements of a runaway robot.

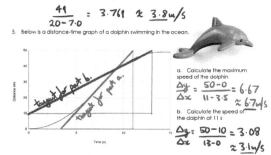

a. Calculate the robot's maximum speed

$$v = s/t = 24/4.0 = 6.0 \, m/s$$

b. Calculate the robot's minimum speed when moving

$$v = s/t = 4.0/4.0 = 1.0 \, m/s$$

c. Calculate how long the robot was stationary for

$$2.0 + 5.0 = 7.0 \, s$$

d. Calculate the average speed of the robot **only when it is moving** i.e. not including the time the robot is stationary

$$\frac{49}{20-7.0} = 3.769 \approx 3.8 \, m/s$$

5. Below is a distance-time graph of a dolphin swimming in the ocean.

tangent for part b.
tangent for part a.

a. Calculate the maximum speed of the dolphin

$$\frac{\Delta y}{\Delta x} = \frac{50-0}{11-3.5} = 6.67 \approx 6.7 \, m/s$$

b. Calculate the speed of the dolphin at 11 s

$$\frac{\Delta y}{\Delta x} = \frac{50-10}{13-0} = 3.08 \approx 3.1 \, m/s$$

GCSE
VELOCITY-TIME GRAPHS

Velocity-time graphs show us an object's velocity over time. They can also be used to work out the acceleration and the total displacement of an object.

1. Write down the equations for acceleration and displacement.

$$a = \frac{v-u}{t} \qquad s = vt$$

2. State what the gradient and area under a velocity-time graph represent respectively.

$$a = \text{gradient} \qquad s = \text{area under the graph}$$

3. Below is a velocity-time graph for a swordfish swimming in the ocean.

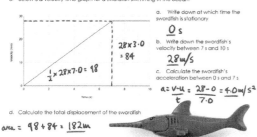

a. Write down at which time the swordfish is stationary

$$0 \text{ s}$$

$$28 \times 3.0 = 84$$

b. Write down the swordfish's velocity between 7 s and 10 s

$$28 \text{ m/s}$$

$$\tfrac{1}{2} \times 28 \times 7.0 = 18$$

c. Calculate the swordfish's acceleration between 0 s and 7 s

$$a = \frac{v-u}{t} = \frac{28-0}{7.0} = 4.0 \text{ m/s}^2$$

d. Calculate the total displacement of the swordfish

$$\text{area} = 98 + 84 = 182 \text{ m}$$

Below is a different velocity-time graph for the same swordfish on a different swim.

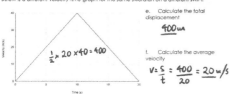

e. Calculate the total displacement

$$400 \text{ m}$$

$$\tfrac{1}{2} \times 20 \times 40 = 400$$

f. Calculate the average velocity

$$v = \frac{s}{t} = \frac{400}{20} = 20 \text{ m/s}$$

gcsephysicsonline.com/**motion-graphs**

---

4. This is a velocity-time graph of an alien spaceship.

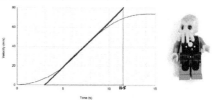

a. Calculate the average acceleration of the spaceship over 15 s

$$a = v-u/t = \frac{74-0}{15} = 4.133 \approx 4.9 \text{ m/s}^2$$

b. Calculate the maximum acceleration of the spaceship (steepest gradient)

$$\text{gradient} = \frac{\Delta y}{\Delta x} = \frac{80-0}{11.5-3.0} = 9.412 \approx 9.4 \text{ m/s}^2$$

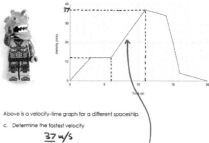

Above is a velocity-time graph for a different spaceship.

c. Determine the fastest velocity

$$37 \text{ m/s}$$

d. Calculate which spaceship has a greater maximum **positive** acceleration

$$a = \frac{v-u}{t} = \frac{37-12}{5} = +5.0 \text{ m/s}^2$$

The _first_ spaceship had the greatest positive acceleration.

gcsephysicsonline.com/**motion-graphs**

GCSE
EQUATIONS OF MOTION

The following worksheet is based on the relationship between the initial and final velocities of an object, its acceleration and the distance it travels.

final velocity² - initial velocity² = 2 x acceleration x distance

1. Name the units that each of the four variables in the equation are measured in.

$$\text{m/s} \qquad \text{m/s} \qquad \text{m/s}^2 \qquad \text{m}$$

2. Write down the equation using symbols rather than words.

$$v^2 - u^2 = 2as$$

3. i) Rearrange the equation to make **v** the subject. ii) rearrange to make **u** the subject. iii) rearrange to make **a** the subject and iv) rearrange to make **s** the subject.

i) $$v = \sqrt{u^2 + 2as}$$

ii) $$u = \sqrt{v^2 - 2as}$$

iii) $$a = \frac{v^2 - u^2}{2s}$$

iv) $$s = \frac{v^2 - u^2}{2a}$$

4. Fill in the table with the missing values (to 2 sf).

v (m/s)	u (m/s)	a (m/s²)	s (m)	Calculations
37	0	12	56	$v = \sqrt{0^2 + (2 \times 12 \times 56)} = 36.661$
19	5.0	2.5	67	$v = \sqrt{5.0^2 + (2 \times 2.5 \times 67)} = 18.974$
23	22	3.4	7.8	$u = \sqrt{23^2 - (2 \times 3.4 \times 7.8)} = 21.817$
12	8.1	10	3.9	$u = \sqrt{12^2 - (2 \times 10 \times 3.9)} = 8.124$
120	20	20	350	$a = (120^2 - 20^2)/2 \times 350 = 20$
79	0.10	66	47	$a = (79^2 - 0.10^2)/2 \times 47 = 66.394$
450	2.3	32	3200	$s = (450^2 - 2.3^2)/2 \times 32 = 3200$

gcsephysicsonline.com/**v-squared**

---

5. A boxer goes for a run to improve her fitness. She starts at rest and slowly but constantly accelerates to a sprinting velocity of 7.0 m/s in a time of one and a half minutes.

a. Calculate the boxer's acceleration

$$a = \frac{v-u}{t} = \frac{7.0-0}{90} = 0.0777 \approx 0.078 \text{ m/s}^2$$

b. Calculate the total distance travelled by the boxer

$$s = \frac{v^2 - u^2}{2a} = \frac{7.0^2 - 0}{2 \times 0.0777} = 315 \approx 320 \text{ m} \ (2 \text{ sf})$$

6. A dog escapes from its owner's front garden. The dog moves at an initial velocity of 3.0 m/s then accelerates at 1.4 m/s² over a distance of 58 m. (2 sf)

a. Calculate the dog's final velocity

$$v = \sqrt{u^2 + 2as} = \sqrt{3.0^2 + (2 \times 1.4 \times 58)}$$
$$= 13.09 \approx 13 \text{ m/s}$$

The dog reaches the speed calculated in part a. and runs out of energy. It immediately starts to slow down until it stops and lies down having travelled a further distance of 39 m.

b. Calculate the dog's deceleration from maximum speed to rest

$$a = \frac{v^2 - u^2}{2s} = \frac{0^2 - 13.09^2}{2 \times 39} = -2.197 \approx -2.2 \text{ m/s}^2$$

c. Write down the total distance covered by the dog during its escape

$$58 + 39 = 97 \text{ m}$$

The owner, travelling on their bike, accelerates from rest until they get to the position of the resting dog, reaching a final velocity of 10 m/s at this point.

d. Calculate the owner's acceleration

$$a = \frac{v^2 - u^2}{2s} = \frac{10^2 - 0^2}{2 \times 97} = 0.5155 \approx 0.52 \text{ m/s}^2$$

As the owner reaches the dog, they slam the brakes on hard, causing them to come to a complete stop. The brakes cause a deceleration of 8.4 m/s².

e. Calculate the distance covered by the owner as they decelerate

$$s = \frac{v^2 - u^2}{2a} = \frac{0^2 - 10^2}{2 \times -8.4} = 5.952$$

$$\approx 6.0 \text{ m}$$

gcsephysicsonline.com/**v-squared**

GCSE
NEWTON'S SECOND LAW

The acceleration of an object is dependent on the force acting on it and its mass.

$$F = ma$$

1. Write down the equation in words rather than symbols and name the units that each of the three variables in the equation are measured in.

$$(\text{resultant}) \; force = mass \times acceleration$$
$$N \qquad kg \qquad m/s^2$$

2. Write down a different equation for acceleration in terms of initial and final velocities.

$$a = \frac{v - u}{t}$$

3. Calculate the force acting on the following:

a. A 20 kg mass being accelerated at 3.0 m/s²

$$F = ma = 20 \times 3.0 = \underline{60 \, N}$$

b. A 0.70 kg mass being accelerated at 20 m/s²

$$F = ma = 0.70 \times 20 = \underline{14 \, N}$$

c. A 60 g mass being accelerated at 20 km/s²

$$F = ma = 0.060 \times 20\,000 = \underline{1200 \, N}$$

d. A 130 kg mass being accelerated from rest to 50 m/s in 25 s

$$a = \frac{v-u}{t} = \frac{50-0}{25} = 2.0 \, m/s^2 \qquad F = ma = 130 \times 2.0 = \underline{260 N}$$

4. Rearrange the first equation i) to make **m** the subject, then ii) to make **a** the subject.

i) $m = \dfrac{F}{a}$ ii) $a = \dfrac{F}{m}$

5. Fill in the table with the missing values.

Force (N)	Mass (kg)	Acceleration (m/s²)	Calculations
20	80	0.25	$F = ma = 80 \times 0.25 = 20$
800	80	10	$a = F/m = 800/80 = 10$
800	20	40	$a = F/m = 800/20 = 40$
800	80	10	$m = F/a = 800/10 = 80$
1.00	9.11×10^{-31}	1.098×10^{30}	$m = F/a = 1.00/1.098 \times 10^{30}$

this is actually the mass of an electron in kg

6. The average human has a mass of 75.0 kg.

a. Calculate the weight of the average human (use g = 9.80 N/kg for this question)

$$W = mg = 75.0 \times 9.80 = \underline{735 \, N} \; (3sf)$$

The 'average' human jumps from a diving board into a swimming pool. Their weight provides the resultant force that accelerates them

b. Ignoring air resistance, calculate their acceleration

$$a = \frac{F}{m} \qquad F = W \qquad a = \frac{735}{75.0} = \underline{9.80 \, m/s^2}$$

A 3.50 g LEGO minifigure is dropped at exactly the same time. Calculate:

c. The weight of the minifigure

$$W = mg = 3.50 \times 10^{-3} \times 9.80 = \underline{0.0343 \, N}$$

d. The resultant force of the minifigure

$$F = 0.0343 \, N \; (\text{ignoring air resistance})$$

e. The acceleration of the minifigure

$$a = \frac{F}{m} = 0.0343 / 3.50 \times 10^{-3} = \underline{9.80 \, m/s^2}$$

f. Compare you answers from part b. to part e.

Their acceleration is the same, even though they have a different mass.

7. A teenager has just passed their driving test. They borrow their mum's car to see how fast it will accelerate from 0 – 60 mph (equal to 27 m/s).

a. It takes them 9.0 seconds. Calculate their acceleration

$$a = \frac{v-u}{t} = \frac{27-0}{9.0} = \underline{3.0 \, m/s^2}$$

b. The car has a mass of 1.2 tonnes. Calculate the average resultant force

$$F = ma = 1200 \times 3.0 = \underline{3600 \, N}$$

They lose control at 60 mph and hit a lamp post causing the car to come to a complete stop in a time of 0.75 s.

c. Calculate the deceleration of the car

$$a = \frac{v-u}{t} = \frac{0-27}{0.75} = \underline{-36 \, m/s^2}$$

GCSE
STOPPING DISTANCES

The distance it takes for a vehicle to come to a stop is dependent on both the reaction time of the driver (which affects the thinking distance) and the braking distance of the vehicle.

1. Define the stopping distance of a vehicle.

The total distance travelled by a vehicle after the driver sees a hazard and the vehicle comes to a complete stop.

2. The stopping distance of a vehicle is the sum of two different distances.

a. Name and describe one of the distances

Thinking distance - the distance travelled before the brakes are applied.

b. Name and describe the other distance

Braking distance - the distance travelled after the brakes are applied.

3. Write down four reasons why a driver's reaction time might be delayed.

Tiredness, distractions (including mobile phones), alcohol and drugs.

4. As well as the driver's capacity to react, write down and explain something else that the thinking distance is dependent on.

The initial speed of the vehicle.

5. Imagine a car is braking. Write down three things that might affect the braking distance.

Surface of the road (wet or icy), condition of the tyres and condition of the brakes.

6. Write down the equation for stopping distance in terms of the two distances given as answers in question 2.

Stopping distance = thinking distance + braking distance

7. Briefly describe an experiment to test the reaction time of a person.

Drop a ruler through the finger of a test subject.

Record the distance that the ruler falls, this is related to the reaction time of the person.

8. Write down the equation for speed in terms of distance and time.

$$v = \frac{s}{t}$$

9. Hence write down the proportionality relationship between distance and speed while the driver reacts to put the brakes on (reaction time).

$$v \propto s \qquad or \qquad s \propto v$$

10. Write down the equation for the kinetic energy of the car travelling at velocity, v.

$$E_k = \frac{1}{2} m v^2$$

11. Describe the relationship between the initial kinetic energy of the car and the work done by the brakes on the wheels.

$$W = E_k$$

12. A student claims that stopping distance increases linearly with speed. Explain whether their claim is correct or not.

$$W = Fs \qquad E_k = \frac{1}{2} m v^2$$
$$F s = \frac{1}{2} m v^2$$
$$\therefore \; s \propto v^2$$

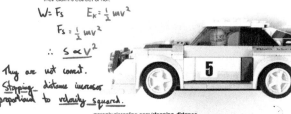

They are not correct. Stopping distance increases proportional to velocity squared.

GCSE
MOMENTUM

Momentum can be thought of as the quantity of motion that an object possesses. It is dependent on an object's mass and its velocity.

momentum = mass x velocity

1. Name the units that each of the three variables in the equation are measured in.

$$kg\,m/s \qquad kg \qquad m/s$$

2. Write down the equation using symbols rather than words.

$$p = mv$$

3. Calculate the momentum of:

   a. A 4.0 kg mass with a velocity of 8.0 m/s

   $$p = mv = 4.0 \times 8.0 = \underline{32\ kg\,m/s}$$

   b. An 8.0 kg mass with a velocity of 4.0 m/s

   $$p = mv = 8.0 \times 4.0 = \underline{32\ kg\,m/s}$$

   c. An 8.0 kg mass with a velocity of 8.0 m/s

   $$p = mv = 8.0 \times 8.0 = \underline{64\ kg\,m/s}$$

4. i) Rearrange the equation to make **m** the subject and ii) rearrange to make **v** the subject.

   i) $$m = \frac{p}{v}$$ ii) $$v = \frac{p}{m}$$

5. Fill in the table with the missing values to 3 sf.

p (kg m/s)	m (kg)	v (m/s)	Calculations
46.8	13.0	3.60	$p = mv = 13.0 \times 3.60 = 46.8$
358	28.2	12.7	$p = mv = 28.2 \times 12.7 = 358.14$
340	67.0	5.07	$v = p/m = 340/67.0 = 5.0746$
268	14.4	18.6	$v = p/m = 268/14.4 = 18.611$
80.0	0.625	128	$m = p/v = 80.0/128 = 0.625$
18.6	31.0	0.600	$m = p/v = 18.6/0.600 = 31$

---

6. A barbeque that has a mass of 32 kg is left outside during a hurricane. The strong wind causes the barbeque to travel at 0.90 m/s.

   a. Calculate the barbeque's momentum

   $$p = mv = 32 \times 0.90 = 28.8 \approx \underline{29\ kg\,m/s} \quad (2\cancel{sf})$$

The lid of the barbeque comes off and blows away. The lid has the same momentum as calculated in part a, but has a mass of 3.5 kg.

   b. Calculate the barbeque lid's velocity

   $$v = \frac{p}{m} = \frac{28.8}{3.5} = 8.2286 \approx \underline{8.2\ m/s}$$

7. A satellite has a mass of approximately 1.2 tonnes and travels at 7.0 km/s.

   One tonne = 1000 kg

   a. Calculate the satellite's momentum

   $$p = mv = 1200 \times 7000 = \underline{8.4 \times 10^6\ kg\,m/s} \quad (2\cancel{sf})$$

Because space is a vacuum, objects such as meteoroids can travel at very high velocities. A meteoroid with a mass of 120 kg has the same momentum as the satellite.

   b. Calculate the velocity of the meteoroid

   $$v = \frac{p}{m} = \frac{8.4 \times 10^6}{120} = \underline{70\,000\ m/s}$$

   c. Display the ratio of the satellite's and the meteoroid's:

   i) masses $$1200 : 120 \qquad \underline{10 : 1}$$

   ii) velocities

   $$7000 : 70000 \qquad \underline{1 : 10}$$

The meteoroid, which orbits the sun, has a constant speed, equal to the velocity calculated in part b.

   d. Explain why the momentum of the meteoroid is constantly changing

   The direction of the meteoroid is constantly changing, so its velocity and momentum (which are vector quantities) are also constantly changing.

GCSE
CONSERVATION OF MOMENTUM

Momentum, like energy, is always conserved. In a closed system, the total sum of momentum before an event, like a collision, always equals the total sum of momentum after the event.

$$p_{before} = p_{after}$$

1. Write down the equation for the momentum of an object.

$$p = mv$$

2. Complete the equation showing the relationship of two colliding objects with masses m_1 and m_2, initial velocities u_1 and u_2 and final velocities v_1 and v_2.

$$p_{1,before} + p_{2,before} = p_{1,after} + p_{2,after}$$

$$m_1 u_1 + m_2 u_2 = m_1 v_1 + m_2 v_2$$

3. Calculate the total momentum of:

   a. A 2.0 kg mass and a 7.0 kg mass both travelling at 4.0 m/s in the same direction

   $$p_{total} = p_1 + p_2 = m_1 v_1 + m_2 v_2 = (2.0 \times 4.0) + (7.0 \times 4.0)$$
   $$= \underline{36\ kg\,m/s}$$

   b. A 0.20 kg mass travelling at 120 m/s and an 80 kg mass travelling at 0.80 m/s in the same direction

   $$p_{total} = p_1 + p_2 = m_1 v_1 + m_2 v_2 = (0.20 \times 120) + (80 \times 0.80)$$
   $$= \underline{88\ kg\,m/s}$$

   c. A 4.0 kg mass and a 3.0 kg mass both travelling at 8.0 m/s but in opposite directions

   $$p_{total} = p_1 + p_2 = m_1 v_1 + m_2 v_2 = (4.0 \times 8.0) + (3.0 \times -8.0)$$
   $$= \underline{8.0\ kg\,m/s}$$

   d. A 5.0 kg mass travelling at 12 m/s travelling in one direction and a 20 kg mass travelling at 3.0 m/s in the opposite direction

   $$p_{total} = p_1 + p_2 = m_1 v_1 + m_2 v_2 = (5.0 \times 12) + (20 \times -3.0)$$
   $$= \underline{0\ kg\,m/s}$$

---

4. Two sixth formers are playing rugby. One player has a mass of 70 kg and is travelling at 4.0 m/s. He collides with the other player (on his own team) who has a mass of 100 kg and is at rest.

   a. Calculate the total momentum of the two players

   $$p_{total} = p_1 + p_2 = m_1 u_1 + m_2 u_2$$
   $$= (70 \times 4.0) + (100 \times 0) = \underline{280\ kg\,m/s}$$

After the impact, the two students move off together.

   b. Calculate the final velocity of the two students

   $$v = \frac{p}{m} = \frac{280}{(70+100)} = 1.647 \approx \underline{1.6\ m/s} \quad (2\,sf)$$

Later in the game, they collide again. This time the 100 kg student travels at 5.0 m/s and collides with the 70kg student who is at rest. After the collision, the 100 kg student stays at rest.

   c. Calculate the final velocity of the 70 kg student

   $$m_1 u_1 + m_2 u_2 = m_1 v_1 + m_2 v_2 \qquad 500 = 70 v_2$$
   $$(100 \times 5.0) + (70 \times 0) = (100 \times 0) + (70 \times v_2) \qquad v_2 = 7.143$$
   $$\approx \underline{7.1\ m/s}$$

5. Mary is surfing in Devon. She has a mass of 59 kg (including her board) and catches a wave which causes her to travel at a velocity of 5.5 m/s.

   a. Calculate Mary's momentum

   $$p = mv = 59 \times 5.5 = 324.5 \approx \underline{320\ kg\,m/s} \quad (2\,sf)$$

A dolphin swims alongside Mary as they both travel at 6.8 m/s. The total combined momentum of the dolphin and Mary is 1140 kgm/s.

   b. Calculate the dolphin's mass

   $$p = m_1 v_1 + m_2 v_2$$
   $$1140 = (59 \times 6.8) + (m_2 \times 6.8)$$
   $$1140 - 401.2 = 6.8 m_2 \qquad m_2 = 108.65 \approx \underline{110\ kg}$$

Mary catches a different wave. This wave propels her at 7.6 m/s but the dolphin swims directly at her at 5.1 m/s. The dolphin jumps out of the water and collides with Mary (luckily both are unhurt).

   c. Calculate the resulting velocity of both the dolphin and Mary if they 'stick' together after the collision

   $$m_1 u_1 + m_2 u_2 = (m_1 + m_2)v$$
   $$(59 \times 7.6) + (108.65 \times -5.1) = (59 + 108.65)v$$
   $$v = -0.63057 \approx \underline{-0.63\ m/s}$$
   (opposite direction to Mary)

GCSE
WAVE CALCULATIONS

The velocity (or speed) of a wave can be calculated
by multiplying frequency by wavelength.

velocity = frequency x wavelength

1. Write down the equation using symbols rather than words.

$$v = f\lambda$$

2. Write down the equation describing the relationship between the frequency and the time period of a wave.

$$\text{frequency} = \frac{1}{\text{time period}} \qquad f = \frac{1}{T} \quad or \quad T = \frac{1}{f}$$
capital T for time period

3. Calculate the velocity of:

   a. A wave with a wavelength of 12 m and a frequency of 3.0 Hz

   $$v = f\lambda = 3.0 \times 12 = \underline{36 \text{ m/s}}$$

   b. A wave with a wavelength of 0.10 m and a frequency of 120 Hz

   $$v = f\lambda = 120 \times 0.10 = \underline{12 \text{ m/s}}$$

   c. A wave with a wavelength of 1.0×10^{-6} m and a frequency of 3.0×10^{14} Hz

   $$v = f\lambda = 3.0 \times 10^{14} \times 1.0 \times 10^{-6} = \underline{3.0 \times 10^{8} \text{ m/s}}$$

   d. Explain what type of wave travels at the same velocity as the wave in part c.

   Electromagnetic waves (including light) in a vacuum

4. i) Rearrange the wave speed equation to make λ the subject, then ii) rearrange to make f the subject.

   i) $$\lambda = \frac{v}{f}$$ ii) $$f = \frac{v}{\lambda}$$

5. Fill in the table with the missing values.

Velocity (m/s)	Wavelength (m)	Frequency (Hz)	Calculations
3.0×10^{8}	1.0×10^{7}	30	$v = f\lambda = 30 \times 1.0 \times 10^{7} = 3 \times 10^{8}$
3.0×10^{8}	6.4×10^{-5}	4.7×10^{12}	$\lambda = v/f = 3.0 \times 10^{8} / 4.7 \times 10^{12} = 6.383 \times 10^{-5}$
330	0.015	2.2×10^{4}	$\lambda = v/f = 330 / 2.2 \times 10^{4} = 0.015$
3.0×10^{8}	1.2×10^{-6}	2.5×10^{14}	$f = v/\lambda = 3.0 \times 10^{8} / 1.2 \times 10^{-6} = 2.5 \times 10^{14}$
14.2	499	0.0285	$f = v/\lambda = 14.2 / 499 = 0.02846$

2sf —
3sf —

6. Batman is developing some sonar technology for his echolocation goggles. He stands in a cave holding a speaker and a timer 99.0 m away from the far end of the cave. Batman remembers that sound travels at about 330 m/s in air.

   a. Calculate the time the sound waves take to travel to the far end and back

   $$v = \frac{s}{t} \qquad t = \frac{s}{v} = \frac{99 \times 2}{330} = 0.600 \text{ s} \quad (3 \text{ sf})$$

The sound wave completes 1,200 wave cycles in the time it takes to travel to the far end and back.

   b. Calculate the time period of one wave cycle

   $$\frac{0.600}{1200} = 5.00 \times 10^{-4} \text{ s}$$

   c. Hence, calculate the frequency of the sound wave

   $$f = \frac{1}{T} = \frac{1}{5.00 \times 10^{-4}} = \underline{2000 \text{ Hz}}$$

   d. Hence, calculate the wavelength of the sound wave to 2 sf

   $$\lambda = \frac{v}{f} = \frac{330}{2000} = 0.165 = \underline{0.17 \text{ m}}$$

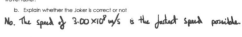

7. The Joker is developing some high-powered torches for his fight against Batman. He reads that the torch has a frequency of 5.30×10^{14} Hz and a wavelength of 5.66×10^{-7} m.

   a. Show that the speed of light is about 3.00×10^{8} m/s

   $$v = f\lambda = 5.30 \times 10^{14} \times 5.66 \times 10^{-7}$$
   $$= 299\,980\,000 \approx 3.00 \times 10^{8} \text{ m/s}$$

The Joker claims that if he increases the frequency, then he could make the light travel faster.

   b. Explain whether the Joker is correct or not

   No. The speed of 3.00×10^{8} m/s is the fastest speed possible.

The Joker wants to produce light in the infrared zone at a wavelength. λ = 950 nm.

   c. Calculate the frequency of this infrared light (1 nm = 1 x 10^{-9} m)

   $$f = \frac{v}{\lambda} = \frac{3.00 \times 10^{8}}{950 \times 10^{-9}} = 3.158 \times 10^{14}$$
   $$= \underline{3.16 \times 10^{14} \text{ Hz}} \quad (3 \text{ sf})$$

GCSE
REFLECTION

If a wave meets a boundary between two materials and cannot be transmitted through, it is either absorbed or bounced back into the material (medium) it has come from. This is reflection.

angle of incidence = angle of reflection

1. Explain what specular reflection means.

    This is when the reflected ray is in one direction only.

2. Explain what diffuse reflection means.

    This is when the wave is reflected in multiple directions.

3. Give a reason why specular reflection can be more dangerous than diffuse reflection.

   An intense laser beam could be reflected into an eye, causing permanent damage.

4. Draw a diagram of a beam of light reflecting off a plane mirror. Include labels for the normal, the angle of incidence, the angle of reflection and the mirror. Ensure you show the direction the light is travelling.

   normal
   angle of incidence   angle of reflection
   i r
   mirror

5. Complete the reflection diagram below and, using a protractor, measure the angle of incidence and the angle of reflection.

   $$i = r = 54°$$

   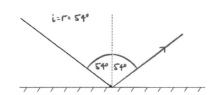
   54° 54°

---

6. Complete the reflection diagram below and continue until the light escapes the mirrors.

7. Complete the reflection diagrams below. label which is specular reflection and which is diffuse reflection.

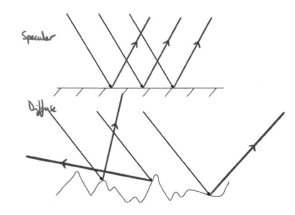

Specular

Diffuse

GCSE
ULTRASOUND SCANNING

Sound waves with a frequency above the range of human hearing are called ultrasound.

1. Write down the frequency limits for human hearing.

   20 – 20,000 Hz

2. Explain why humans have an upper limit for the frequency of sound they can hear.

   Limitations in how quickly the eardrum can vibrate.

3. Describe some differences between sound waves and electromagnetic waves.

   EM - Faster (3.0×10^8 m/s), can travel through a vacuum and are transverse waves.

4. Write down the approximate speed of sound in air (at standard pressure and temperature).

   About 330 m/s

5. Sound can also be used for echolocation. If we know the speed of sound and we measure the time it takes for the sound to be emitted, reflect off the object and return, we can calculate the distance.

   a. Write down the equation for speed, in terms of distance and time

   $$v = \frac{s}{t}$$

   b. Rearrange the above equation for distance

   $$s = vt$$

   c. Explain why the above equation does **not** give the distance to an object using echolocation

   This is the distance there and back.

6. Give an example and explain why it is useful for ultrasound to be only **partially** reflected. **This allows the wave to continue to travel and reflect off multiple objects. Eg in scanning babies.**

7. Describe how the received ultrasound signal differs from the emitted signal.

   It is less intense.

8. Give an example where echolocation is used in nature.

   Bats use it to hunt their prey.

gcsephysicsonline.com/**ultrasound**

---

9. Ultrasound is used for scanning pregnant women.

   a. Describe if there any risks posed by the use of ultrasound scanning

   No, it is safe.

   b. Name some advantages of using ultrasound for pregnant women compared with other methods of seeing inside the body, such as X-rays for example

   It does not use ionising radiation which could harm the developing baby.

The frequency of ultrasound used in imaging is approximately 2.0 MHz.

   c. Assuming the speed it travels through tissue is 1600 m/s, calculate the wavelength of the ultrasound

   $$\lambda = v/f = 1600/2.0 \times 10^6 = 8.0 \times 10^{-4} \text{ m}$$

The ultrasound source is placed on the skin of a pregnant woman during a scan so waves only travel tens of centimetres. This means they return very quickly. We assume the speed of sound is the same as in question c.

   d. Calculate the time that the ultrasound takes to be emitted, reflected off a boundary 20 cm from the scanner and received back

   $$t = \frac{s}{v} = \frac{2 \times 0.20}{1600} = 2.5 \times 10^{-4} \text{ s}$$

The ultrasound waves are not fully reflected, they are partly transmitted and partly reflected.

   e. Describe how the computer is able to build a picture of the baby using ultrasound scanning

   Thousands of data points are collected every second, building a picture of the distances to various parts of the baby which is displayed as an image.

$1 \text{ ms} = 1 \times 10^{-3} \text{ s}$

10. Ultrasound echolocation can be used by engineers to locate defects in long pipes. The ultrasound signal is sent down a pipe. The receiver receives two signals, one after 90 ms (the defect) and the other after 135 ms (the end of the pipe).

   Calculate the distance between the **end** of the pipe and the defect

   2 s

   Speed of waves in pipe = 5 000 m/s

   $$s_{defect} = \frac{vt}{2} = \frac{5000 \times 90 \times 10^{-3}}{2} = 225 \text{ m}$$

   $$s_{end} = \frac{vt}{2} = \frac{5000 \times 135 \times 10^{-3}}{2} = 337.5 \text{ m}$$

   $$337.5 - 225 = 112.5$$
   $$= 110 \text{ m} \quad (2 \text{ s.f.})$$

gcsephysicsonline.com/**ultrasound**

GCSE
ELECTROMAGNETIC WAVES

The electromagnetic spectrum consists of all the possible wavelengths and frequencies of electromagnetic radiation, including visible light.

1. Put the following types of electromagnetic radiation in order from the smallest wavelength to longest wavelength.

Microwave	Gamma	Ultraviolet	X-ray	Visible Light	Radio	Infrared
6	1	3	2	4	7	5

2. State the velocity of all electromagnetic (EM) waves in a vacuum.

   3.00×10^8 m/s

3. Identify the type of EM radiation that transfers the most energy.

   Gamma (highest frequency)

4. EM waves are the only waves that can travel through a vacuum

   a. (True)   b. False

5. State the type(s) of EM wave(s) that can be used in communication.

   Radio, micro, IR and visible.

6. Write down what FM, LW and MW stand for in terms of radio communications.

   Frequency modulation, long wave and medium wave.

7. Compare microwaves to radio waves when used for communications.

   Microwaves do not spread out as much so can be used with satellites, but radio waves spread out around hills.

8. State the type of EM radiation that every object emits. **So they can easily be detected.**

   Infrared.

9. Name the seven colours that make up visible (white) light from shortest to longest wavelength.

   Violet, indigo, blue, green, ~~~ orange and red.

10. Visible light has a wavelength range of approximately 400 nm – 700 nm. Calculate the approximate range of frequencies for visible light (1 nm = 1 × 10⁻⁹ m).

   $$f = v/\lambda = 3.0 \times 10^8 / 400 \times 10^{-9} = 7.5 \times 10^{14} \text{ Hz}$$

   $$f = v/\lambda = 3.0 \times 10^8 / 700 \times 10^{-9} = 4.3 \times 10^{14} \text{ Hz}$$

   Range from 4.3×10^{14} to 7.5×10^{14} Hz

gcsephysicsonline.com/**em-spectrum**

---

11. EM radiation with a wavelength less than that of visible light can be damaging to skin cells because it is ionising. Name the three types of EM radiation this corresponds to.

   UV, X-ray and gamma.

12. Explain why ionising radiation can be harmful to animals and humans.

   It can cause mutations in the DNA in cells.

13. Write down some uses we have for X-rays.

   Scanning for broken bones.

14. Explain why radiographers stand behind a protective screen when they take an X-ray.

   To reduce their exposure to the ionising X-rays.

15. Explain how X-rays can be produced.

   By decelerating electrons.

16. Match the EM radiation to the object they are absorbed by.

Microwave	Gamma	Ultraviolet	X-ray	Visible light
Skin	Water molecules in food	Several metres of lead	Black cloth	Bone

17. Describe how microwaves heat up food.

   It causes (water) molecules to vibrate more so the food heats up.

18. Calculate the wavelength of EM radiation that has a frequency of 2.3 × 10¹⁵ Hz.

   $$\lambda = \frac{v}{f} = \frac{3.0 \times 10^8}{2.3 \times 10^{15}} = 1.3 \times 10^{-7} \text{ m}$$

19. Calculate the frequency of EM radiation that has a wavelength of 9.8 × 10⁻⁹ m.

   $$f = \frac{v}{\lambda} = \frac{3.0 \times 10^8}{9.8 \times 10^{-9}} = 3.1 \times 10^{16} \text{ Hz}$$

gcsephysicsonline.com/**em-spectrum**

GCSE
REFRACTION

As a wave passes over the boundary between one medium and another it changes speed. If the wave is not travelling exactly perpendicular to the boundary then it will also change direction.

1. Describe how the angle of refraction differs from the angle of incidence if the wave speeds up as it crosses a boundary.

As the wave speeds up, the angle of refraction increases.
r > i

2. Write down i) the colour of light that refracts the most and ii) the colour of light that refracts the least.

i) *Violet*   ii) *Red*

3. A wave can be thought of as being made up of parallel wavefronts, one wavelength apart. Use this description of waves to explain in detail why refraction occurs.

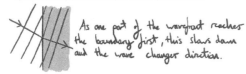

As one part of the wavefront reaches the boundary first, this slows down and the wave changes direction.

4. The diagram on the right shows a light ray incident on a perspex block.

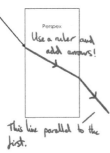

Use a ruler and add arrows!

   a. Write down whether the light will speed up or slow down as it crosses the boundary from air to perspex

   Slow down.

   b. Write down whether the light will speed up or slow down as it crosses the boundary from perspex to air

   Speed up.

   c. Hence, complete the diagram as light travels from air, through a perspex block and out into air again

   This line parallel to the first.

5. Complete the diagram showing where a light ray refracts at the surface of two glass blocks.

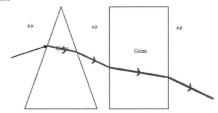

6. Double glazed windows can sometimes fill up with water if there is a leak. Complete the diagram showing where a light ray refracts at the surfaces of air, glass and water. Light travels fastest in air, then water and slowest in glass.

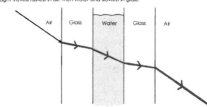

7. Explain, in terms of refraction, and by completing the diagram, why shining a beam of white light at a triangular prism produces a beam of light that is all the colours of the rainbow. Use your answer to question 2.

White light is made up of many other colours of light. Red has the longest wavelength and refracts the least, while violet has the shortest wavelength and refracts (bends) the most.

(This is called dispersion)

GCSE
CONVEX (CONVERGING) LENSES

A convex (or converging) lens uses refraction to bend light in order to either focus (cameras) or disperse (magnifying glass) light.

1. Describe the shape of a convex lens.

Fatter in the middle.

2. Write down the name of the point in space that a convex lens focuses light to.

The focal point.

3. Write down the name of the distance between the centre of a convex lens and the point named in question 2 above.

The focal length.

4. Describe what happens to light that passes through the centre of a convex lens.

It continues on in a straight line.

5. Complete and the following diagrams below for light from an object being focused by a convex lens.

   a.

Image

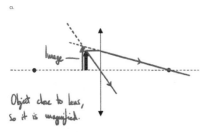

Object close to lens, so it is magnified.

b.

c.

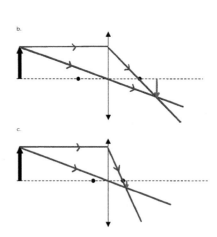

6. Describe the image produced of an object with a convex lens (include the image's size, orientation, position and whether or not it is real or virtual) when:

   a. The object is less than one focal length from the lens

   Magnified, upright, same side as the object and virtual.

   b. The object is a long way from the lens

   Smaller, upside down, on the other side of the lens and real.

GCSE
CONCAVE (DIVERGING) LENSES

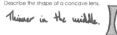

A concave (or diverging) lens uses refraction to bend light in order to diverge (or spread out) light incident on it.

1. Describe the shape of a concave lens.

    Thinner in the middle.

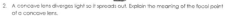

2. A concave lens diverges light so it spreads out. Explain the meaning of the focal point of a concave lens.

    This is the point, on the other side of the lens, where the rays appear to come from.

3. Explain what is meant by a virtual image.

    Formed by a virtual ray of light.
    (this means it can't be projected onto a screen)

4. Explain how we can see a virtual image if it is in fact, virtual.

    We can observe it when we look through the lens. It is where the rays of light appear to come from.

5. Complete and label the following diagrams below for light from an object being diverged by a concave lens:

    a.

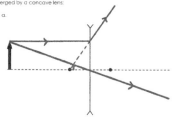

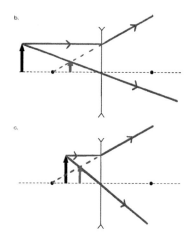

b.

c.

6. Describe the image produced by a concave lens when the object is at a distance greater than the focal length. Include the image's size, orientation, position and whether or not it is real or virtual.

    Smaller, upright, closer to the lens and virtual.

7. Compare how your answer for question 8 would be different if a convex (converging) lens was used instead of a concave (diverging) lens. See your convex lens worksheet for guidance.

    Both images smaller, but the image from a convex lens would be upside down and real.

GCSE
COLOUR

The range of colours we see around us are our brain's perception of light (electromagnetic radiation) with different colours corresponding to different wavelengths and frequencies.

1. In Physics, the three primary colours of light are slightly different from those taught when painting in Art. Write these 3 colours down.

    Red, green and blue.

2. Write down the three secondary colours of light and what combination of primary colours makes them.

    Cyan, magenta

3. Write down what colour is made when all three primary colours are combined in equal proportion.

    White.

4. Explain if the same occurs when all three secondary colours are combined in equal proportion.

    Yes it does, as all the colours of light are mixed.

5. Explain how a yellow light source and a blue light source can make white light when combined.

    is made from red and green, so when added to blue there are all three primary colours of light.

6. Explain why a tree appears green (ignoring GCSE Biology).

    It reflects green light from the white light that shines on it.

7. Describe what a colour filter does and how it works.

    It allows that colour through and absorbs all the other colours.

8. Write down what colour a tree would appear if looked at through a green filter.

    Green

9. Write down what colour a tree would appear if looked at through a red filter.

    Black

10. One of the first people to investigate colour theory was Italian Leonardo da Vinci. The Italian flag is shown below. Sketch the Italian flag if it was observed as follows:

    Green -   - Red

    a. Through a red filter

    b. Through a green filter   c. Through a blue filter

11. Complete the drawings below showing white light reflected from a surface. Complete the ray diagram and label the colour of light reflected.

    a. White surface   White light

    b. Blue surface   Blue only

    c. Black surface   No colours reflected

GCSE
MAGNETIC FIELDS

Every magnet has a magnetic field around it. Within the magnetic field, other magnets and magnetic materials experience a force.

1. Write down the names given to the two ends of a magnet.

    North and south poles

2. Write down which end of a magnet a compass points to.

    The south pole

3. Describe how Earth's magnetic field is vital for life to exist on Earth.

    It deflects charged particles from the Sun, these would be harmful to life on Earth.

4. Traditional bar magnets are an example of a permanent magnet. Explain what is meant by a permanent magnet.

    It remains magnetic

5. A magnetic field can be displayed using field lines. Write down the direction that field lines point in.

    From N to S

6. Sketch the shape of a magnetic field around a bar magnet.

     lines going from N to S

7. Explain what it represents when magnetic field lines are close together.

    The field there is stronger

8. Explain what it means when a magnet's field lines are parallel and equally spaced out.

    This represents a uniform field
    This means it's the same everywhere

gcsephysicsonline.com/**magnets**

9. A moving charged particle will produce a magnetic field. Hence explain why a current flowing through a wire produces a magnetic field.

    An electrical current is the movement of negative electrons - these produce the magnetic field.

10. Explain what a solenoid is.

    A coil of wire (that can carry a current)

11. Describe the shape of a solenoid's magnetic field, including inside and outside the solenoid and where the field is strongest.

    Similar to the shape around a bar magnet, inside the coil it is a uniform field.

12. Explain why an iron core is often placed in a solenoid.

    This increases the strength of the magnetic field.

13. Draw the magnetic field lines around the following magnetic objects:

    a. Current carrying wire (conventional current going into the page)

    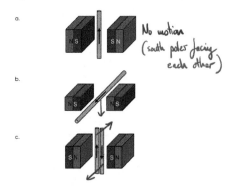

    Concentric circles (ideally you'd use a compass and a pencil)

    b. The Earth

    Field lines pointing towards the top

gcsephysicsonline.com/**magnets**

GCSE
THE MOTOR EFFECT

A wire that carries current through an external magnetic field experiences a force at right angles to both the current flow and the magnetic field. We use Fleming's left hand rule to determine in which direction this force acts.

1. Below is a picture of the hand position for Fleming's left hand rule. Label each of the fingers/arrows with what they represent.

    force / movement
    magnetic field
    conventional current

2. Describe the direction of the three variables relative to each other i.e. the angle between them.

    They are all at 90° to one another.

3. In a permanent magnetic field explain how the force on a current carrying wire changes if the current changes direction.

    If the current changes direction, the force also changes direction.

Below is the equation for the force acting on a current carrying wire in a magnetic field.

$$F = BIL$$

4. Write down the equation using words rather than symbols and name the units that each of the four variables in the equation are measured in.

    Force = Magnetic Field Strength × Current × Length
    N   T (tesla)   A   m

5. Calculate the force acting on the following:

    a. A 10 cm wire with a current of 2.0 A in a magnetic field of 0.45 T

       F = BIL = 0.45 × 2.0 × 0.10 = 0.090 N

    b. A 2.0 m wire with a current of 10 A in a magnetic field of 8.0 T

       F = BIL = 8.0 × 10 × 2.0 = 160 N

    c. A 2.0 m wire with a current of 10 kA in a magnetic field of 8.0 mT

       F = BIL = 8.0 × 10⁻³ × 10 × 10³ × 2.0 = 160 N

gcsephysicsonline.com/**motor-effect**

6. Below are three diagrams of current carrying wires within a magnetic field. Use Fleming's left hand rule to determine the direction of motion of each wire.

    a. 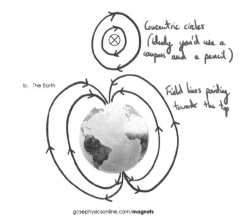 No motion (south poles facing each other)

    b.

    c.

7. Describe the parts of a simple electric motor.

    • Permanent magnets - to provide the magnetic field
    • A coil of wire - wrapped around an armature
    • Axle for it to rotate about and a commutator

8. Explain the role of a split ring commutator in a DC motor and how it enables the motor to spin continuously in the same direction.

    This changes the direction of the current every 180° of rotation.

9. Explain how a loudspeaker uses the motor effect to produce sound waves.

    A coil of wire, attached to a cone, can move relative to a circular magnet. Depending on the direction of the current this moves the cone in or out. By altering the current rapidly this causes the cone to vibrate, producing a sound wave.

gcsephysicsonline.com/**motor-effect**

GCSE
THE GENERATOR EFFECT

The generator effect can be thought of as the opposite of the motor effect: by moving a conductor in a magnetic field we can induce a potential difference and hence a current.

1. Compare the similarities and differences between the motor and generator effects.

Motor - a current in a magnetic field causes movement
Generator - movement in a magnetic field causes a current

2. Describe a way of generating a current using a wire and permanent magnet.

Move a wire, connected to a circuit, relative to the magnet.

3. Write down three things that would induce a greater potential difference and therefore a greater current.

Stronger magnet, move the wire faster and have a greater number of turns on a coil of wire.

4. Describe what happens when a plastic object falls through a copper tube.

It just falls through (with a small amount of friction)

5. Explain why a magnet falling through a copper tube falls very slowly.

The moving magnet induces a current in the copper, this current generates its own magnetic field which then repels the original magnet.

6. Alternators and dynamos are two types of generators. Describe the main difference between them.

Alternators - AC   Dynamos - DC

7. Describe the shape of an alternating current (AC) graph with respect to time.

A sinusoidal curve   often called a sin curve

8. Describe how we can increase the amplitude of the AC output.

Stronger magnet
Rotate faster
More turns on the coil   NOT more coils!!!

---

9. Describe how we can decrease the frequency of the AC output.

Rotate the coil slower

10. Speakers and microphones are often thought of as very different. Describe how speakers and microphones are actually quite similar.

Similar - Both have a coil next to a permanent magnet

Different - Speakers - current causes motion
Microphone - motion causes current

11. Mains electricity runs at 230V and is an alternating current source. Write down the frequency of mains AC.

50 Hz   in the UK

12. Sketch the graph of potential difference against time for a generator if under the following conditions:

a. The magnetic field strength is doubled

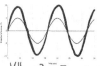

Voltage × 2   Freq = Same

b. The coil is rotated half as quickly

Voltage × ½   Freq × ½

c. The magnet direction is reversed

Voltage = opposite   Freq = same

d. The coil is rotated twice as quickly **and** the magnetic field strength is halved

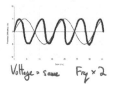

Voltage = same   Freq × 2

GCSE
TRANSFORMERS 1

Transformers are used to reduce the power loss in the national grid. Below is an equation for power loss in a current carrying wire.

$$P = I^2R$$

1. Write down the equation using words rather than symbols and name the units that each of the three variables in the equation are measured in.

Power = Current² × Resistance
W   A   Ω

2. Calculate the power loss of:

a. 10 A flowing through a 270 Ω resistor

$$P = I^2R = 10^2 \times 270 = 27000 \text{ W}$$

b. 1.0 A flowing through a 270 Ω resistor

$$P = I^2R = 10^2 \times 270 = 270 \text{ W}$$

3. Explain the effect of reducing the current through a wire.

This reduces the power loss

Decrease I by ×10 and this decreases P ×100

4. A simple transformer includes an iron core and two separate coils of wire. Describe how this apparatus is put together to produce a transformer.

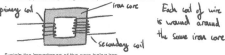

primary coil   iron core   secondary coil

Each coil of wire is wound around the same iron core

5. Explain the importance of the core being iron.

Iron is magnetically 'soft' so can be demagnetised quickly.

6. Describe the magnetic field produced by a coil of wire carrying an alternating current.

It is a constantly changing (alternating) magnetic field.

---

7. Describe in order, the steps that cause an alternating current in one coil to produce an alternating current in a second coil. (Think about the magnetic field, potential difference and current of both coils).

• A changing current in the primary coil causes a changing magnetic field inside it
• This causes the iron core to become magnetised, so a changing magnetic field is also inside the secondary coil
• This changing magnetic field induces a potential difference across the secondary coil - and therefore a current in the secondary circuit

An equation used with transformers is:

$$V_p/V_s = n_p/n_s$$

8. Write down the equation using words rather than symbols and name the units that each of the four variables in the equation are measured in.

$$\frac{\text{potential difference in primary coil}}{\text{potential difference in secondary coil}} = \frac{\text{no. turns on primary}}{\text{no. turns on secondary}}$$

9. In a step-down transformer the number of turns in the primary coil is 980 compared to the secondary coil which only has 175. The output is 1.0 kV, calculate the input voltage.

$$V_p = \frac{n_p}{n_s} \times V_s = \frac{180}{175} \times 1000 = 5600 \text{ V}$$
$$(5.6 \text{ kV})$$

10. The number of turns in a primary coil of a transformer is 135. The transformer steps the voltage up from an input of 12.5V to 230V. Calculate the number of turns in the secondary coil.

$$n_s = n_p \times \frac{V_s}{V_p} = 135 \times \frac{230}{125} = 2484$$
$$\simeq 2480 \text{ turns}$$
$$(3 \text{ sf})$$

GCSE
TRANSFORMERS 2

The ratio of potential differences across two coils of wire in a transformer is dependent on the ratio of the number of turns of both coils. This affects the ratio of currents in each coil.

1. Write down the meaning of the law of conservation of energy.

Energy cannot be created or destroyed

Therefore ∴ Energy in = Energy out

2. Explain how the law of conservation of energy applies to conservation of power.

Power in = Power out $\left(P = \dfrac{E}{t}\right)$

3. Write down the equation for electrical power in terms of current and potential difference (voltage).

$P = VI$

4. In a transformer, there are two separate circuits, each with its own potential difference and current. Write down how the power of the two circuits are related in an ideal transformer (the power in the primary coil, P_p, and the power in the secondary coil, P_s)

$P_p = P_s$

5. Hence derive an equation relating the potential difference and current of both primary and secondary coils.

$V_p I_p = V_s I_s$ $\dfrac{V_p}{V_s} = \dfrac{I_s}{I_p}$

6. Explain how increasing or decreasing the potential difference across one circuit affects that circuit's current.

Increasing $V \rightarrow$ decreases I (provided the power
Decreasing $V \rightarrow$ increases I remains constant)

7. Household electrical items use transformers in their chargers. A phone charger transforms mains electricity to 5.2 V and 8.6 A. Calculate the current drawn in the mains (230 V) when the phone is plugged in.

$I_p = \dfrac{V_s\ I_s}{V_p} = \dfrac{5.2 \times 8.6}{230} = 0.19443$

$\simeq \underline{0.19\ A}$
$(2sf)$

gcsephysicsonline.com/**transformers**

8. A transformer has a primary current of 210 A, a secondary current of 7.6 A and a secondary voltage of 1.9 kV. Calculate the primary voltage.

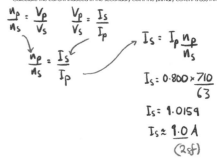

$V_p = \dfrac{V_s\ I_s}{I_p} = \dfrac{1900 \times 7.6}{210} = 68.762$

$\simeq \underline{69\ V}$

9. The ratio between the number of turns in the primary coil of a transformer to the secondary coil is 85. Calculate the secondary voltage if the primary voltage is 1700 mV.

$\dfrac{n_p}{n_s} = \dfrac{V_p}{V_s}$ $V_s = V_p \dfrac{n_s}{n_p} = 1700 \times 10^{-3} \times \dfrac{1}{85}$

$= 0.02$

$\dfrac{n_p}{n_s} = 85$ $\dfrac{n_s}{n_p} = \dfrac{1}{85}$ $\simeq \underline{0.020\ V}$ $(2sf)$

10. Explain why transfers are used in the National Grid.

To step-up the voltage to a really high value so the current in the cables is as low as possible. This reduces the heating effect and energy losses.

11. The primary coil in a transformer has 710 turns whilst the secondary coil has 63. Calculate the current induced in the secondary coil if the primary current is 800 mA.

$\dfrac{n_p}{n_s} = \dfrac{V_p}{V_s}$ $\dfrac{V_p}{V_s} = \dfrac{I_s}{I_p}$

$\dfrac{n_p}{n_s} = \dfrac{I_s}{I_p}$ $I_s = I_p \dfrac{n_p}{n_s}$

$I_s = 0.800 \times \dfrac{710}{63}$

$I_s = 9.0159$

$I_s \simeq \underline{9.0\ A}$
$(2sf)$

gcsephysicsonline.com/**transformers**

GCSE
LIFECYCLE OF STARS

All stars are born in the same way but there are many different ways in which they end their lives, depending on their mass.

1. State the most abundant element in the Universe.

Hydrogen

2. Describe what a nebula is.

A star forming region of dust and gas.   mainly hydrogen and a small amount of helium

3. Hot, dense regions form in nebulas. State what these regions are called.

Protostars

4. State the process that binds hydrogen nuclei together.

(Nuclear) fusion   this is called 'radiation pressure'

5. Explain how the answer to question 4 prevents a star from collapsing.

There is an outward force from the fusion that balances the force of gravity acting inwards.

6. Describe how hydrogen nuclei (protons) undergoing fusion can produce helium nuclei (2 protons and 2 neutrons).

Through a number of reactions, 4 protons join to make one helium nuclei. 2 protons change to neutrons.
You don't need to know the full details of this for GCSE

7. Describe what happens to an average star when the hydrogen fuel starts to run out and what it uses as fuel instead.

It starts to fuse heavier elements, like helium, as it becomes a red giant.

8. Describe what happens to an average sized star once all the fuel has run out.

The red giant shrinks until it becomes a white dwarf. (Eventually it will cool to become a black dwarf)

9. Explain why a more massive star has a shorter life than a smaller star.

The force of gravity is greater so it uses up its fuel quicker.

gcsephysicsonline.com/**stars**

10. Write down the heaviest element that a massive star can form during its main sequence.

Iron (Fe)

11. Explain why some elements cannot be produced by fusion in main sequence stars.

Elements, including uranium, are heavier than iron so cannot be made by fusion in stars.

12. Explain how the elements that cannot be produced in main sequence stars are produced.

They are formed when a massive star collapses in a supernova. At this time the conditions are so hot and energetic it allows fusion of really heavy elements.

13. State what is left behind after a supernova if the mass of the remaining material is so great that it cannot support itself.

A black hole

14. Write down what is at the centre of our galaxy, the Milky Way.

A super massive black hole — our Solar System is orbiting this

15. State the volume, in metres cubed, of a black hole.

$0\ m^3$ A black hole has a really high mass but zero volume!

gcsephysicsonline.com/**stars**

It all started with a Big Bang!

1. Describe how we can split white light into a spectrum of colours.

Using a prism (or a diffraction grating)

2. Describe what an absorption spectrum is. ▓▓ | | ▓ spectral lines

This shows the wavelengths of light absorbed by a particular element or compound.

3. Explain what the black lines in a star's absorption spectrum tell us about the star.

These tell us about the types of elements or compounds found in the atmosphere of that star.

4. Explain why a galaxy's absorption spectrum might be shifted, and to what end of the spectrum it is shifted towards.

It is shifted because that galaxy is moving relative to us. This is towards the red end of the spectrum.

5. Describe the relationship between a galaxy's distance from us and how much its light is redshifted by.

The greater the distance the greater the redshift.

6. If every galaxy's absorption spectrum is redshifted, explain what this tells us about the Universe.

That all the galaxies are moving away from each other, so the Universe must be expanding.

7. If the Universe is expanding, explain why this is one piece of evidence for the Big Bang.

Previously the Universe must have been smaller. If you go far back enough in time then it must have started at a single point.

8. State what CMBR stands for.

Cosmic Microwave Background Radiation

9. Explain what the expansion of the Universe has done to this radiation.

It has stretched it from a short wavelength to the longer wavelength of microwaves.

10. Explain why CMBR is a further piece of evidence for the Big Bang.

As the Universe has expanded, so too has this radiation that was around at the time of the Big Bang.
Big Bang   Now

11. Explain what will happen to the wavelength of the CMBR in the future as the Universe keeps expanding.

It will continue to increase.
← Future →

12. Describe the evidence for dark matter.

When observing stars in galaxies their movement cannot be explained based on the mass of the stars that we can see – there must be something else.

13. Write down what is actually happening to the rate of expansion of the Universe.

It is increasing!

14. Describe the evidence for dark energy.

Dark energy is responsible* for this increasing rate of expansion of the Universe.

* we currently believe

Revising for exams needs to be well structured and planned. Use this notebook to help with your preparation for your GCSEs.

GCSE PHYSICS

EXAM REVISION NOTES

Lewis Matheson

A LEVEL
PHYSICS

DAILY WORKOUT

Year 1: July - October

Lewis Matheson

BOOK 1

PhysicsOnline.com   ▶ Physics Online

Thinking about A Level Physics? This
workbook is an ideal way to prepare for
the course before you start your A Levels.

PHYSICS ONLINE

LEWIS MATHESON

I'm a former **Physics Teacher** and Head of Science, I began making videos to support students back in 2015. Now, I have established websites specialising in GCSE and A Level Physics as well as hugely popular channels on YouTube and TikTok.

Furthermore, I continue to work with many organisations to support teachers, including the Royal Academy of Engineering, Ogden Trust, Institute of Physics, and STEM Learning.

WEBSITES AND SCHOOL SUBSCRIPTIONS

Hundreds of schools now have full access to dedicated websites for both **GCSE** and **A Level Physics** – everyday thousands of students access high-quality videos whenever they need them; these videos include practical experiments, livestreams, worked examples, and regular updates about exams.

Have a look at **GCSEPhysicsOnline.com** to find out more about a **Premium Plan** or **School Subscription** to the website.

Printed in Great Britain
by Amazon

16449589R00102